Christ Woman

Wisdom and Victory
For Women Serving the Lord

*"And the armies in heaven,
clothed in fine linen, white and clean,
followed Him on white horses."*
~Revelation 19:14~

Diana Scheich

Go Tell Ministries
Louisville, Kentucky
USA

ISBN 978-1-4675-3380-5

Dedication

**Jesus Christ, Soon-Coming
King of Kings & Lord of Lords**

My Mother, Sheila Graham Veth

My Daughter, Laura Lynn Baum

My Daughters-in-law, Lauren Joy Risinger
and Laura Leigh Scheich

My Granddaughters, Kelsey Louise,
Heidi Alexa and Emma Lee

All Christ Women everywhere who long
to serve and worship Him in spirit and truth

Appreciation

My daughter, Laura, on the cover
and for her photography
and assistance in graphic art.

Dr. Roger and Becky Hoagland for the
photo shoot using Faith,
their magnificent horse.

Dear friends, Al and Jean Fazio,
and Debbie Zupances
for their many hours of editing.

Susan Glass, for her constant
encouragement and help in reprinting this book.

Faithful and dear friends who have
contributed to Go Tell Ministries.

TABLE OF CONTENTS

TABLE OF CONTENTS

Introduction

*"And it shall come to pass in the last
days, says God, that I will pour out of My
Spirit on all flesh; your sons and your
daughters shall prophesy...and on My
maidservants I will pour out My Spirit in
those days; and they shall prophesy..."*
~Joel 2:28, Acts 2:17-18~

These are the "last days" spoken of by the
prophets, the disciples and Jesus Christ.
God's Son proclaimed that He would
come back at the end of the age and that
He would have a mighty end-time army.
Many women are part of that end-time
army. They have answered His call, *"Who
will go for me? Who will I send?"* His
mighty women are preparing themselves,
understand authority, and are forming
rank. They are "Christ Women."

I was raised in a traditional Christian
church but left it at the age of eighteen. I
didn't leave because of problems with the
church but because of abandoning a
commitment to God and choosing to go
my own way in life. After five years of one
disappointment after another, my whole
world fell apart.

Disillusioned with myself and other
people, I decided there was probably not
a God at all and continued on a journey

1

of self destruction. After another year of dead ends and frustration, I met a wonderful man who began to tell me about his Christian experience. He told me stories of faith and about the importance of being saved and filled with the Spirit of God. As he talked, something stirred deeply within my heart, and a hunger developed to discover more about his faith.

It wasn't long before he invited me to church. On a chilly night in December 1970, I reluctantly stepped through the front doors and into the hallway leading to the sanctuary of Evangel Tabernacle. A large banner hung on the wall over the platform declaring, "The Church Where Everybody is Somebody and Jesus is Lord!"

A warm feeling of love and peace began to wrap itself around my cold and lonely heart. Friendly people with sincere, broad smiles shook my hand and made me feel instantly at home. As we were seated, beautiful music began to fill the air and soon the congregation stood, opened their hymnals and started to worship. On that glorious night, a depressed, rejected and lost young woman heard the Gospel of salvation preached in a way she could finally understand; and she responded by inviting Jesus Christ to be her Lord and Savior for the rest of her life. The man who invited me to church was Joe Scheich.

On September 1, 1972, Joe and I were married at Evangel Tabernacle in Louisville, Kentucky where we had been born again. It was a time of joyful new beginnings. We couldn't wait to start a life together serving the Lord.

Joe was always very outgoing, but I was shy and liked to stay in the background. However, my desire to reach out to others with the Gospel of Jesus Christ helped me to overcome a very timid nature and step out to fulfill the destiny God had ordained for my life. I wanted to shout from the housetops, "I used to be miserable and made so many mistakes. My life seemed to have no purpose, and I even wanted to die. Then one day Jesus Christ became real to me. Jesus saved me and wondrously filled me with His Holy Spirit. Now I am full of God's love, joy and peace. Let me tell you how to have the same experience!"

Joe and I have had an amazing journey our entire married life. We have hosted hundreds of home prayer meetings, taught and preached in churches, jails and prisons, on street corners and in foreign lands.

By God's grace, He has enabled me to serve Him for many years in various capacities within the church: Missions Director and Associate Pastor, Chaplain and Bible teacher at a Christian high school, dean of a Bible college, co-host of a Christian television program and author of books. Along this wondrous path, there were not many mature women teaching the younger women about successfully serving in the ministry, while often juggling a number of other responsibilities. Most lessons I learned the hard way—but learned well.

At this stage in my life, God has placed a strong impression on my heart to pass the wisdom He has taught me over the years to the next generation. The Father desires that younger women learn from the mothers who have gone before them, so they will be spared many heartaches and problems. By no means has my life been perfect and without regrets, mistakes and failures. However, all is not lost if one learns from such experiences. Wisdom is gained and character refined.

It is my prayer that every woman who seeks to serve Christ will be blessed in some way from the lessons of one woman's life in the service of the Lord Jesus Christ.

Diana Scheich

~1~
The Secret Place
The King and You

*"Those who stay in God's presence
don't have to enter God's presence."*
~Unknown~

It was the cool of the evening. The first "perfect" day of the year was gently going to sleep as I walked across the church parking lot. An evening class had just begun; and I had stopped by to tell the women hello. It gave me joy and satisfaction to see the new college—specifically for women called to ministry—going so well. Ladies of all ages and backgrounds were excited to learn more about topics that would equip them in the work of the ministry.

The sun had just disappeared over the horizon; a light breeze brushed my face. All of a sudden, He let me know He was there. Jesus walked at my right side. I looked at Him and smiled.

One of my most beloved and personal Scriptures comes from Acts 2:25:

"For He is at my right side and will not be moved." The Holy Spirit revealed to me that Jesus is always with me. When this first happened, questions filled my mind. How could it be? There are billions of people on the earth, infinite numbers of spiritual beings, major events happening all over the world, urgent prayer requests from multitudes of people and end-time matters needing constant attention. This is not to mention all of the "important" Christians on God's front lines needing Him more than one woman about His business on a much smaller scale.

Being God, He is omnipresent, He fills heaven and the earth and even the depths of hell. But that seems so imper-sonal. How could He, Jesus Christ, the "express image of the Father" walk with me, an ordinary Christian?

More thoughts raced through my mind about all of the times I had failed...missed it...grieved His Holy Spirit...not "been there for Him" having been caught up in myself and my plans. A deep sigh escaped my lips and my heart sank.

Then He spoke. Oh, those wonderful, glorious and often unexpected times when He speaks! They are engrained for-ever in my heart.

"Daughter, did I not say in my

Word, 'In My Father's House are many mansions?' In My heart, there are many rooms. All of My children have their very own room. It is theirs alone, and no one else may enter. You have your own special room in My heart, and it is yours alone. I keep you there always. You invited me into your heart; and from that moment, you were in mine also. Did I not say that you are in Me, and I am in you, and we are in the Father? Your room will never belong to another. I really do love you and always have."

Love and joy flooded my soul and a new level of peace. Now it was easier to understand. I looked over at Him, as we continued walking, and smiled again. "Jesus, I love you so much." He seemed to take my hand as we continued walking.

"But, Jesus, I wanted to do so much for you and worked so hard; in reality, I've accomplished very little. It hurts me so."

His soul touched mine and He whispered, "What I want more than anything is for you to love Me. Just love Me. Be with Me."

We were silent for awhile. Everything else disappeared. Then He spoke again, "The vision will be fulfilled."

(The "vision" is the plan for my life

that God showed me many years ago. God has a vision—a plan—for everyone's life. Few find it and, sadly, many don't care.)

Jesus is our "hiding place," our "cleft in the rock," our "stream in the desert." He wants you to know there is a room in His heart with *your* name on it. It belongs only to *you,* and no one else can ever take your place. It's impossible to understand how He can love so many or care about our every thought and need. He hasn't called us to understand, just to believe and receive His Word.

Close your eyes now, lean your head back and meditate on His promise, *"I am at your right side and I will not be moved."*

Do you sense His presence? He is there. Listen and He will speak.

That is what I do every time something difficult must be done and anxiety tries to attach itself to my heart. I just shut my eyes and immediately sense His presence, His strength, His love and know He will get me through. Not only will He get me through, but He will be glorified as His strength is made perfect in my weakness.

Remember this always, you are never alone. He is always there, patiently waiting for your trust and invitation.

6 Truths About Your Secret Place

1. It is kept beautiful with love— *"You shall love the Lord your God with all your heart, with all your soul, and with all your mind" (Matthew 22:37).*
2. It is kept clean with holiness— *"...But as He who called you is holy, you also be holy in all your conduct, because it is written, 'Be holy, for I am holy'" (1 Peter 1:15-16).* The Greek word for *holy* (*hagios*) means, "...sacred, pure, blameless...consecrated...Godlikeness..." (Strong's # 40).
3. It is comfortable because it is lived in— *"Every day I will bless You, and I will praise Your name forever and ever" (Psalm 145:2).* You will never lose your awe and respect of His Majesty; but the more time you spend with Him, the easier it is to relax and share together.
4. It is a safe place— *"Thou callest in trouble, and I delivered thee in the **secret** place of thunder..." (Psalm 81:7 KJV).* When you are with Him, you are in the center of God's will which is the safest place in all of creation. At times, you

may go through persecutions and trials. Many Christians have even been martyred for their faith; yet they never leave His Hand, and they are never alone or abandoned. In the midst of his testing, Job proclaimed with great and unshakable faith, *"though He slay me, yet will I trust Him" (Job 13:15).*

5. It is disturbed by fear, anger and other negative thoughts and emotions— *"Finally brethren, whatever things are true, whatever things are noble, whatever things are just, whatever things are pure, whatever things are lovely, whatever things are of a good report, if there is any virtue and if there is anything praiseworthy—meditate on these things" (Philippians 4:8).* When we allow our hearts to descend into the world of bad thoughts and the resulting disturbed emotions, we lose our peace. When we lose our peace, we cannot sense His presence; even worse when we sin, He seems to be far away. We feel unworthy to call out to Him and may be ashamed. The truth is that He never leaves us. But our consciences must be clear and clean before we can enjoy sweet fellowship with Jesus again.

6. Jesus will share the Father's heart with you and give you revelation and instructions on living a successful and

meaningful life— *"In the* **secret places** *of the cliff, let me see your face, let me hear your voice; for your voice is sweet, and your face is lovely" (Song of Solomon 2:14).* We, as believers, strive to walk with the Lord and enjoy His presence at all times. It is rewarding beyond words to set aside a special time each day to sit at His feet. If we listen carefully, He will speak loving words of life to us.

It has been during such intimate times with the Lord that He has shown me things to come, given me assignments and divine instructions and also has corrected me. There have also been those times when my heart was crushed and my soul seemed overwhelmed beyond hope. When no one else seemed to understand or considered my pain and loneliness, He has always been there.

He will comfort you.
He will love you.
You will be satisfied.

"He shall hide me in His pavilion, in the **secret place** *of His tabernacle He shall hide me..." (Psalm 27:5).*

"He who dwells in the **secret place** *of the Most High shall abide under the shadow of the Almighty" (Psalm 91:1).*

~2~
Discover Your Divine Destiny

"Never lose the opportunity of urging a practical beginning, however small, for it is wonderful how often in such matters the mustard seed germinates and roots itself."
~Florence Nightingale~

You were born with a purpose. You were not an accident to God. It is possible that your parents did not plan you. Maybe they wanted you and maybe they did not.

The important fact is that God, at the moment of your conception, by His Holy Spirit breathed upon you and gave you life. From that second, you had a purpose. You had a destiny.

By design of God, your spirit was birthed in a tiny body. He hovered over you in the womb and was intricately involved in your development. Your Heavenly Father gave you gifts and talents that are unique. Out of the nearly eight billion people on the earth today—

14

and all others who have been created or will be created—there is something you can do that no one else can do. There is someone you can reach with the love of God that no one else can reach. No one else can be the person you were created to be.

You have a very important purpose.
You must discover it.
You must fulfill it.

God gave it to you and He will give you the means to complete His vision for you. If you do not find your destiny and flow in it, you will never be happy or at peace within yourself. A square peg will never be comfortable in a round hole.

You must be willing to do whatever it takes and pay the price to reach the dreams and assignments which He gives you.

"But you formed my inward parts; you covered me in my mother's womb. I will praise you because I am fearfully and wonderfully made; marvelous are your works, and that my soul knows very well. My frame was not hidden from you when I was made in secret. Your eyes saw my substance, being yet unformed. And in Your book they all were written, the days fashioned for me, when as yet there were none of them" (Psalm 139:13-16).

In 1820, an African-American girl was born a slave in Dorchester County, Maryland. With no rights, education or opportunities, her future looked dim indeed. But the little girl had "heart."

All through her childhood, Harriet Tubman endured gross mistreatment. Through it all, she remained courageous and compassionate. While still an adolescent, she was sent to the store for supplies and encountered a slave from another owner fleeing for his freedom. His overseer closed in on him and demanded Harriet to help stop the runaway. She refused. The angry overseer threw a rock at the slave running away but hit Harriet in the head instead. The wound was grievous and she nearly died.

Did all of those persecutions and trials keep her from pursuing her destiny? Absolutely not! Drawing from her deep faith in Christ, Harriet eventually escaped from her cruel owner. For the rest of her life, Harriet, nicknamed "Moses," risked her life many times helping hundreds of slaves escape and find freedom in the north. This great woman, who loved God with all of her heart, lived a long life greatly respected and revered.

Her name and story is recorded in history as a woman who received her assignment from God and would not back down or give up regardless of the opposition.

Somehow, you have instinctively known there is a reason for your being. When you were a child you wondered about the future, had dreams and desires and longed for the day when you would be mature enough to walk into your grown-up life where your dreams and destiny would be beautifully and wondrously completed. Now as an adult, you may feel bewildered, but you do not have to speculate anymore.

"I know the thoughts that I think toward you, says the Lord, thoughts of peace and not of evil, to give you a hope and a future" (Jeremiah 29:11).

4 Ways to Discover
Your Destiny

1. What touches your heart with compassion is a clue to your destiny—A young mother tenderly wrapped her baby boy in a soft blanket. Salty tears filled her eyes and ran down her face as she gently stroked his pudgy pink cheek. She held him close and nursed him to the full and prayed to God for divine protection and provision.

Finally, she could wait no longer. Pharaoh's merciless henchmen were getting close and would kill her male child immediately upon discovery. Heart breaking, hands trembling, she covered the tiny basket and sealed it with pitch. Jochebed ran quickly to the bank of the Nile River and carefully pushed the little ark into the awaiting current.

Meanwhile, some distance down the Nile River, Pharaoh's daughter and her attendants approached the waters to bathe. The morning was warm and balmy, and the cool water would be refreshing. As she gazed at the familiar waters, her eyes suddenly noticed a little basket drifting close to the shore. A baby was pitifully crying. Compassion immediately welled up in her heart, and she commanded the baby be brought to her. It only took one look at the handsome child to know she wanted him for her very own.

The rest of the story is well known. Miriam, Moses' sister, had followed the little basket as it floated down the Nile River and was watching when Pharaoh's daughter rescued her baby brother. She courageously offered to find a nurse for the hungry child. Pharaoh's daughter agreed, and Moses' own mother was given the responsibility of caring for him until he was weaned (Exodus 2:1-10).

Rescuing Moses and providing a good education and upbringing for him was the destiny of Pharaoh's daughter. What touches your heart with compassion? It is a key to your destiny.

2. The person who inspires you may be another clue to your destiny—Perhaps, when you were a child, you had a Sunday School teacher who greatly influenced you. One day when she taught about salvation, your heart leapt. As a result of her teaching, you trusted Jesus to be your Savior. For years you have studied the Bible and know it well. Now you have a desire to teach children—but wonder if you have the ability. It has often been said that if God calls you, He will qualify you.

When the prophet Elijah prepared to leave this earth, his faithful assistant, Elisha, would not leave his side. Three times, Elisha begged Elijah not to leave him. When Elijah made it clear that he had to go, he asked Elisha what he could do for him. Elisha didn't ask for silver or gold, but he asked for double Elijah's anointing. God granted his request! (2 Kings 2:7-12).

Elisha was inspired by Elijah so much that he wanted to be used by God in the exact same manner.

3. The problem that needs solving may be a clue to your destiny— Hadassah loved working alongside her cousin's wife. Time for the evening meal was fast approaching. They had been busy about the preparations for hours, grinding the meal, baking the flatbread, roasting the vegetables and meat in the clay outdoor oven. Savory smells wafted through the courtyard. Suddenly, her cousin, Mordecai, ran through the gate with an ashen look on his face and announced, "The king's servants are coming. They want to see Hadassah."

The young, beautiful maiden's face paled. Her heart began to pound. Before the sun set, she entered the king's palace in the citadel of Shushan and was entrusted to a eunuch who was the custodian of women (Esther 2).

How her life had changed in just a few hours! Orphaned at a young age, her cousin and his wife adopted Hadassah to raise as their own daughter. Life had been good even though the Jewish family was living in a Persian land. Due to Mordecai's wisdom, hard work and dependability, he had been promoted to an important position in the king's court. Even though it was a time of relative peace for the thousands of Jewish captives, the hatred and contempt of many Persians toward them was at the point of eruption.

But God had prepared a lovely, young Jewish virgin for a specific time and season. Hadassah quickly won the favor of the keeper of the women with her wit and charm. It pleased him to prepare her with every possible advantage so the king would be delighted when he spent time with her.

So, when the appointed time arrived and the king beheld the exquisitely beautiful and graceful young woman entering his chamber, it wasn't long before he chose her to be his queen and changed her name to Esther meaning "star." And she was truly a star. Under the guidance of her uncle and with many prayers, fastings and supplications, God used her to bring deliverance to the Jewish people in Persia. They were saved from blood-thirsty enemies who would have exterminated all of the Jews.

Esther could have shrank from the plight of her race and turned her head the other way. She could have cried and complained or refused to be drawn into the problem she was called to solve. But her people needed a deliverer, and she made the decision to risk her life and help them.

Someone needs you. There may be a problem only you can solve. It may seem overwhelming. You may feel inadequate. It's your destiny! Say "yes" to the call and see what God will do.

4. The challenges of your past may have uniquely prepared you to fulfill your destiny—In 1944, World War II was raging. Hitler's armies swept across Europe in a mad hunt to gather Jews and annihilate them. A Christian family in Holland, horrified at the plight of their Jewish friends, made the risky decision to hide them until a time of rescue could be arranged. An informant caused the Gestapo to arrest the ten Boom family. Corrie ten Boom's beloved father died ten days later. She and her sister, Betsie, were imprisoned in a horrible German concentration camp. Somehow, Corrie managed to hide a small Bible. In the evenings after hard labor, the women would lie on flea-infested, filthy straw, and Corrie would read to them the Word of God. Barracks 8 became known as "the crazy place where they have hope." More and more women managed to slip into Barracks 8 at night and listened to Corrie read the Scriptures. It is hard to comprehend, but 96,000 women died at Ravensbruck—and Betsie was one of them.

At the end of the war, Corrie was released. Refusing to hold bitterness and unforgiveness, she purposed in her heart to use the terrible experiences to help people know Christ. God opened many doors for her to share her story. In 30 years, she spoke in 61 countries. Her message was always the same:

"No pit is so deep that God is not deeper still."

Maybe you have had horrendous experiences in your past. Perhaps, you have been abused, betrayed, disappointed and rejected. It is possible that you have seen unbearable pain and suffering. Take heart! God can take the worst experiences and turn them into a blessing (Deuteronomy 23:5). In Christ you can never be defeated! When Corrie died at a ripe, old age, these words were carved on her tombstone: "Jesus is our Victory!"

Every gifting and calling is equally honorable and necessary to fulfill God's purposes. We must never be tempted to compare ourselves with others. They may be able to do what we cannot do— but we can do what they cannot do! No matter what your circumstances or challenges, stand up and move forward to fulfill your destiny in Christ!

"I have one desire now—to live a life of reckless abandon for the Lord, putting all of my energy and strength into it."

~Elisabeth Elliot, Wife of
Martyred Missionary Jim Elliot ~

THE OPEN DOOR
I love you, Jesus, more and more.
Thank you for the Open Door.
I see You there and Your Glorious Face
Full of light, love and grace.
Only You know what's on
the other side.
I won't get lost with You as my Guide.

OUR LEGACY

What will be our legacy
When our life comes to an end?
Will our world take notice of our
Demise or even care
Where we have been?

We are painting vivid pictures
On this canvas we call life,
Be it colors that speak of peace
Or ones that cause much strife.
We're writing books read by many,
Without pad or pen or paper –
A novel that tells from beginning to
End, our lives aren't just a vapor.

We do not know the lives we've touched
for good – or, maybe ill;
We have such a tiny span on earth
For our destiny to fulfill.
Eyes are always watching and
Ears hear what we say.
Will what they've heard from our
Lips help them on their way?

Will our words build godly character
That we've spoken to each one,
Or destroy their fragile confidence
From things that we have done?

Our destiny is in our hands,
It starts each day we wake,
We choose the road to travel on
By decisions that we make.
May God give us strength and
Wisdom to live our lives for Him;
To leave imprints of His love
Everywhere we've been.

Our goal should be to carve our
Names on hearts, not slabs of stone,
And pray for a harvest of souls
From seeds that we have sown.
Lord help us guard our hearts
So when we take our final breath,
We'll leave a legacy of love
As we close our eyes in death.

~Donna Riggle~

~3~
The Anointing is For the People

*"But you have an anointing
from the Holy One…"*
~1 John 2:20~

The very word "anointing" is a bit mysterious. Those who have been raised in Christian churches have heard the word often depending on the teachings of their particular denomination. In the Old Testament, the Hebrew word for *anointing* is *mashach.* The description is "rubbing or smearing with oil" and refers to the empowerment of the Holy Spirit to do supernatural things through human vessels. Its most important derivative is *mashiyach* (Messiah), and it appears 39 times in the Bible (the same number of stripes Jesus took on His back).

In the New Testament, the Greek word for *Messiah* is *christos,* and the English translation is Christ. Jesus means "Savior," and Christ means the "Anointed One."

Today, when we speak of God's ministers being anointed, the meaning is they have been endowed with power by the Holy Spirit to do supernatural works of God. Different assignments require different anointings.

Ancient teachings reveal the origin of anointing with oil. When shepherds would take their sheep out to pasture, often flies and other insects would torment the sheep by molesting their eyes. Without help from the shepherds entrusted with their care, the sheep's eyes could easily become infected, and the miserable creatures could possibly go blind. The shepherds discovered if they poured oil over the sheep's heads, the flies would leave them alone.

Isn't it interesting to note the symbolism in this bit of history? Jesus Christ is the Shepherd of His sheep (Christians). One of the names for satan is "Beelzebub" meaning the "lord of the flies." Here we see a picture of the Christian being protected by the Holy Spirit from the attacks of the devil and evil spirits.

In the Old Testament, only judges, kings, prophets and priests were anointed with the holy anointing oil (representing the Holy Spirit) for specific assignments from God.

In the New Testament, the Holy Spirit's anointing is available for every Christian all of the time with no respect to position in the Body of Christ. Revelation 1:6 states that all Christians are "kings and priests" unto God.

Kathryn Kuhlman (1907—1976) was a famous evangelist with a powerful anointing to heal the sick. Thousands of people who needed healing would travel for miles and stand in line for hours to gain entrance into her services. Incredible miracles occurred in the meetings and many were documented by the medical community. Kathryn always gave all the honor and glory to God for His great works. It is said that before her meetings, she would pace back and forth across the floor in her room, praying and crying out to God, "I must have the anointing! I must have the anointing! Oh Father, anoint me again with your Holy Spirit!" Kathryn Kuhlman knew full well that she could not do anything without Him.

All Christians carry the anointing of the Holy Spirit, but not all Christians understand or develop the gift that God has given them. Before His departure from this earth, Jesus comforted His disciples with these words:

"It is to your advantage that I go away: for if I do not go away, the Helper will not come to you; but if I depart, I will send Him to you" (John 16:7).

The anointing of the Holy Spirit is holy and sacred.

- You cannot buy the anointing.
- You cannot fake the anointing.
- You cannot push a button to use the anointing whenever you desire.
- There are no short cuts to the anointing.

At the beginning of His earthly ministry, Jesus arose on the Sabbath and went to the synagogue in His hometown of Nazareth.   He was invited to read a passage of Scripture from the book of Isaiah. All eyes fastened upon Him as He began to read from Isaiah 61:1:

"The Spirit of the Lord God is upon me, because He hath anointed me to preach the Gospel to the poor, he hath sent me to heal the brokenhearted, to preach deliverance to the captives, and recovery of sight to the blind, to set at   liberty them that are bruised..."

All Christians have a mandate from the Lord to continue the works of Christ.

They cannot hope to do so effectively without the anointing of the Holy Spirit.

8 Things to Know About the Anointing

1. THE ANOINTING breaks the yoke (Isaiah 10:27)—In biblical times, yokes were placed around oxen's necks to force them to go the way the driver intended. The yokes were heavy and uncomfortable. Today, yokes refer to heavy burdens with which the enemy weighs us down—such as worries, concerns and the cares of this life. Jesus came to set people free from every yoke of the devil. He broke depression, hopelessness and despair off men and women. His followers have been delegated the same power to set people free in Jesus' Name.

2. THE ANOINTING terrorizes demonic powers (Matthew 8:28-34)—Every time demonized people came into the presence of Jesus, the demons trembled!

When Jesus crossed over the Sea of Galilee to minister in Gadera, a wild, demon-possessed man, who lived in the tombs of the dead, broke loose of the chains holding him, and ran toward

Jesus pleading, *"What do we have to do with you, Jesus, the Son of God? Have you come here to torture us before the time?" (v.29)*.

Jesus proceeded to cast 6,000 demons out of the man into 2,000 pigs feeding nearby. In a frenzied reaction, the swine turned wild and stampeded over a cliff and plunged into the sea!

Jesus gave His followers authority to cast out devils in His Name. There may be times when we are asked to pray for a tormented individual who wants to be set free from an evil power. When this occurs, the best course is to take the person to the church for prayer. If that is not possible, then ask another believer to join with you in prayer for the person who requests help. As you pray in the Name of Jesus, with the anointing of the Holy Spirit, command the demonic spirits to leave. As a Christian, you do not have to fear the enemy.

3. THE ANOINTING will make you bold as a lion (Acts 4:13)—One of the signs of being filled with the Holy Spirit is great boldness. This boldness comes from confidence in Jesus Christ and the power of His Word and His Spirit.

The Apostles Peter and John were common fishermen who did not have the advantage of higher education. However, they had spent three years at the feet of Jesus and had been filled with the Holy Spirit on the Day of Pentecost; they were changed from fearful and unlearned men into anointed and appointed power-ful men of God. When brought before the Jewish Sanhedrin for questioning, the religious leaders were amazed:

"Now when they saw the boldness of Peter and John, and perceived that they were uneducated and unlearned men, they marveled. And they realized they had been with Jesus" (Acts 4:13).

Numerous people were saved, healed and delivered by the hand of God. The church grew quickly and began to spread throughout the Middle East and Asia Minor.

Are you intimidated or apprehensive to speak out for the Lord Jesus Christ? Do you feel unqualified to reach out to people with His love? Spend time with Him through reading the Word and prayer. Worship and adore Him. Invest time with the Savior and His anointing will flow upon you to be His witness.

4. THE ANOINTING empowers you to preach (proclaim) the Good News and set people free (Acts 2)— Once the Holy Spirit came upon the disciples on the Day of Pentecost, the disciples were transformed by the might of God's Spirit. The Holy Spirit anointed men and women who went forth rejoicing while they preached the Good News with gladness. Signs and wonders confirmed the Word of God.

A preacher is one who speaks what he or she believes. In a sense, everyone is a preacher, because every word that comes out of one's mouth speaks out for God, the world system or the evil one.

5. THE ANOINTING is caught by association (1 Samuel 10)—After Saul was anointed by Samuel to be the first king of Israel, he joined a group of prophets as he was returning home. When the prophets began prophesying, the spirit of prophecy came upon Saul, and he also began to prophesy.

With all of your doing, seek to spend time with believers who have strong anointings upon them. On the other hand, avoid close and personal association with those who are not a godly influence on your life. (You are encouraged to witness and minister to them—but do not include them in your intimate circle of fellowship.)

6. THE ANOINTING teaches you all things (1 John 2:27)—If you are full of God's Word and the Holy Spirit, you will not be deceived by false teachers. The

gifts of wisdom and discernment will be
available for whatever you need to do.
However, believers should receive teaching from godly and seasoned men and
women who are ministers of truth.

7. THE ANOINTING must be guarded—
It is the holy power of God and is most
sacred. We are warned not to grieve the
Holy Spirit of God (Ephesians 4:29-32).
Our bodies belong to God, and we are the
temple of the Holy Spirit. There is a price
to pay for the anointing. The price is not
compromising with the world, bearing the
Cross of Christ by crucifying the lusts of
the flesh (Galatians 5:24), equipping one-
self with the Word, sound teaching and
spending much time with the Lord in the
secret place as set out in Chapter 1.

**8. THE ANOINTING you are drawn to
is the anointing you are called to—**In
1910, Agnes Bojaxhiu entered the world
in Skopje, Macedonia. At 12 years of age,
she felt called to give her life to God's
service as a Catholic nun. At age 18,
Agnes began her formal training as a Sister of Loretto and her name was changed
to Sister Theresa.

After some time in the convent, the
Holy Spirit called her to the poor and
dying people of Calcutta, India. Her
authorities were reluctant to grant her
permission. However, she would not give

up and continued asking for their blessing to pursue the call of God on her life. Finally, Sister Theresa was allowed to leave the lovely and peaceful convent in Darjeeling, at the foot of the breathtakingly beautiful Himalayan mountains, to serve the forsaken and rejected people of the hot, crowded and dusty streets in Calcutta.

Few people could understand how the petite young woman, only 28 years of age, could give herself to such a daunting and difficult task. But Sister Theresa tirelessly worked to rescue and care for the sick and dying rejects of society. It wasn't long before many young women wanted to help her. The love and grace that radiated from her presence drew them to the same calling of God. Eventually, a new order was formed—The Missionaries of Charity. Today, Sister Theresa is enjoying her reward in heaven. Before her death at the age of 87, there were over 4,500 sisters and 120,000 co-workers in 133 countries reaching out to orphans and dying homeless people.

There is nothing like flowing in the anointing of the Holy Spirit when you are representing the Lord in word or deed. If you pursue the Anointed One through all of the ways mentioned, one day the anointing of God will be activated within you to fulfill His purposes. Once this happens, you will never want to be without the precious anointing of the Holy Spirit again.

Watch out for pride or thinking you are special because of the anointing that flows through you. The early Christians did not receive the Holy Spirit for their personal self-esteem but for the power to witness Christ (Acts 1:8). The anointing of the Holy Spirit is for power to do works in the Name of Jesus Christ, the Anointed One.

ONLY ONE
You are the Only One
I always want before my face.
You are the Only One
Who saved Me by your grace.
You are the Only One
Who stands at Eternity's Door.
You are the Only One
I want forevermore.

~4~
God's Holy Armor For Women
Rout the Enemy and Possess Your Territory

"It is a poor soldier indeed who does not recognize the enemy."
~Corrie ten Boom~

"Let the high praises of God be in their mouth, and a two-edged sword in their hand" (Psalm 149:6). Glory to God, He gives us weapons to defeat the enemy on every front! It is not for our boasting or attention—but for serious warfare. As we stay spiritually prepared and alert, the Holy Spirit will empower us to be victorious in battle.

"For though we walk in the flesh, we do not war according to the flesh. For the weapons of our warfare are not carnal but mighty in God for pulling down strongholds..." (2 Corinthians 10:3-4).

God's women need not fear the devil or his minions. The truth is they fear the woman of God who knows who she is in Christ.

Jael stepped out of her tent into the humid evening air. She anxiously awaited news of the battle between Sisera, the commander of the Canaanite's army, and Barak who was the commander of Israel's army.

For 20 years, the Canaanites had cruelly oppressed God's people. When the Israelites cried out to God for deliverance, He heard their prayer. He spoke to Deborah, the judge and prophetess of Israel, that it was time to attack and defeat the enemy. Deborah called for war. Barak hesitated to lead a charge against Sisera whose mighty army included 900 iron chariots.

Finally, he agreed to go only if Deborah would go with him. The Israelites defeated the enemy by the mighty hand of the Lord. Sisera fled the battlefield and ran for his life on foot. He thought he would be safe hiding in Heber the Kenite's tent since they were allies.

On that fateful evening, Heber was not at home with his wife, Jael, who was an intelligent, well-informed and courageous woman. She knew that God was for the

Israelites and not the Canaanites.

When Sisera approached her tent, exhausted and afraid, Jael offered him refuge. She gave him milk to drink, and Sisera quickly fell into a deep sleep. Not wasting any time, Jael picked up a tent spike and a mallet. She quietly tiptoed to Sisera's resting place, deftly held the spike over his temple—and with one swift blow, drove it through his head. Sisera died instantly, and Jael was the heroine of the day (Judges 4 and 5).

Christian women need to have the same attitude and courage regarding anything that would dare try to steal or hurt what God has given them. Jesus died, rose from the grave and ascended into heaven. He sent His Holy Spirit to empower believers to win the fight against the devil! *"For this purpose was the Son of God manifested, that He might destroy the works of the devil" (1 John 3:8).*

The Captain of the Lord's Army, Jesus Christ, is calling His women to take their place, fall into rank, and go forth and advance the Kingdom of God.

As soon as we are born again and become Christians, we receive our holy armor for life. But the armor must be used or it will become rusty and not do much good.

It's much like possessing a gun that is loaded and ready to shoot. If an intruder comes into the house and threatens you, the gun will not help lying in the drawer. However, if you take it out of the drawer and fire it straight and steady, it will serve its purpose well.

Let's study the armor of God from a woman's perspective.

THE HELMET OF SALVATION
~Ephesians 6:14~

A helmet covers the head of a soldier. Some helmets cover most of the face also. Openings are provided for the ears to hear, the eyes to see, the nose to breathe and the mouth to speak.

The word *salvation* comes from the Greek word *soterion* and means saved, healed, delivered, restored, liberated and rescued.

The helmet of salvation and all of God's armor is invincible because of its Source of power and protection. When we are born again, we are spiritually covered in the Blood of Jesus. From that point on, God the Father sees us through the shed Blood of His Son as pure and spotless. *"...To Him who loved us and washed us from our sins in His own blood" (Revelation 1:5).*

It is a mystery, but we accept it with great thanksgiving. Satan also sees the Blood and cringes.

"And they overcame him by the blood of the Lamb and by the word of their testimony, and they did not love their lives to death" (Revelation 12:11).

A Christian's salvation provides everything necessary to defeat the enemy and be victorious in battle. There's a time to be meek and mild—and there is a time to fight!

Putting on the Helmet Of Salvation *(Confessions)*

1. I have the mind of Christ (1 Corinthians 2:16b)—This is possible because I study the Bible continually, and His Words have become my constant meditation and influence my thinking. Since I became a Christian, it has been my desire and goal, with the help of the Holy Spirit, to bring every thought captive and in line with biblical principles. Prior to salvation and having been taught the importance of renewing my mind (Romans 12:2), I would let my mind run wherever it wanted to go. However, now that I know my mind is the breeding ground for evil or good, I take the Cross to it and crucify every vain memory, plan and imagination. I reject any thoughts that are ungodly. I will not allow my mind to wander and be lazy.

"...And be constantly renewed in the spirit of your mind—having a fresh mental and spiritual attitude; and put on the new nature (the regenerate self) created in God's image, (Godlike) in true righteousness and holiness" (Ephesians 4:23-24 AMP).

I have decided to see the good in every person and the positive possibilities in every challenge and difficult situation that arises in my life. If I fail (and that happens), I quickly and sincerely ask God to forgive me and move forward with renewed determination.

2. I have wisdom and understanding (Proverbs 1:1-2, James 1:5)—The Spirit of God enlightens my understanding through the Scriptures and revelation. My intelligence and education are important but do not have anything to do with the things of the Spirit. *"The wisdom of man is foolishness with God"* *(1 Corinthians 3:19).*

3. My eyes see things in the spirit as God reveals them to me (2 Kings 6:17)—There is a spirit world all around me, and God will pull back the veil and allow me to see what is necessary.

Gehazi, the servant of Elisha the prophet, was allowed to see chariots of fire and the angels of God. He was greatly encouraged in a fearful situation (see 2 Kings 6:17). In Revelation 3:18, Jesus counseled the church: *"anoint your eyes with eyesalve, that you may see."*

4. My ears hear what the Spirit of God says to me (Revelation 2:7)—Seven times in Chapters Two and Three of Revelation, the churches were exhorted by Jesus to listen to the Spirit of God speaking to them. When I pray, I don't do all of the talking. I am quiet at times and listen for the Spirit of God to whisper instructions to me. *"Be still and know that I am God"* *(Psalm 46:10).*

5. All of my words minister grace to the hearers (Ephesians 4:29)—*"Let no corrupt communication proceed out of your mouth, but that which is necessary for edification, that it may impart grace to the hearers."*

There is an old saying: "If you cannot say something nice about someone, do not say it at all." That saying is based on Scripture. With God's help, I will seek to speak life-giving words to everyone I encounter.

THE BREASTPLATE OF RIGHTEOUSNESS
~Ephesians 6:14~

This crucial piece of armor covers the front of my upper torso, which includes my heart, respiratory and digestive systems, breasts and other vital organs. I am righteous in the sight of God, because I have been redeemed by Christ. (The Greek word for righteousness is *dikaios,* which means holy and innocent. Strong's #1342). It is God's *gift of grace* and cannot be earned by belonging to a certain denomination, doing good works, or any other way. (However, all Christians are exhorted to fellowship and to do good works for the glory of God.)

"For He made Him who knew no sin to be sin for us, that we might become the righteousness of God in Him" (2 Corinthians 5:21).

Putting on My Breastplate (Confessions)

1. The Father and His Son, Jesus, live in my heart (John 14:23)—The heart is the seat of emotions. It is also the place where free will, intellect, wisdom, understanding and conscience intersect. Therefore, I keep my heart undefiled and honor the presence of God. King Solomon exhorted, *"Keep your heart with all diligence for out of it spring the issues of life" (Proverbs 4:23).*

I will not grieve the Holy Spirit by participating in anything that violates His Word. I am not bound by rules and regulations but honor all of God's laws out of love and respect for Him. *"He who loves me will keep my commandments" (John 14:15).*

2. My emotions are under the control of the Holy Spirit—As a mature woman of God, I know it is important to stay "cool, calm, and collected" as I go throughout the day. I want to please the Lord and be a good Christian example at all times. When negative and strong emotions rise up on the inside of me because of something someone says or does—or an unexpected incident occurs— I take a deep breath and ask the

Lord to help me handle myself with restraint and discretion. If necessary, I remove myself from the situation until peace is restored in my heart. Then I will react with wisdom, composure and grace. Furthermore, the hurtful attacks of the devil that would seek to penetrate my heart with offence will bounce right off and have no power to hurt me. The Holy Spirit gives me strength.

"The heart of the righteous studies how to answer; but the mouth of the wicked pours forth evil" (Proverbs 15:28).

GIRDING MY LOINS WITH TRUTH
~Ephesians 6:14~

The "loins" refers to the waist, lower back, and upper and lower abdomen which includes the reproductive organs. The Roman soldier's belt fit closely to the body and held other pieces of the armor together. The truth of God's Word will hold our lives together when nothing or nobody else will.

A scabbard was attached to the belt and in it the sword rested. Often, wide, long leather strips hung down and covered the lower body providing more protection.

How to Gird My Loins With Truth *(Confessions)*

1. The truth of God's Word keeps me from being deceived by any lie of the devil—Romans 1:25 explains that eons ago, mankind *"exchanged the truth of God for the lie..."* People served the devil rather than God. Jesus declared that satan is the "father of lies" in John 8:44. In the opening chapters of Genesis, we read how satan enticed Adam and Eve in the Garden of Eden. Coiled around the forbidden Tree of the Knowledge of Good and Evil, the dazzling creature tempted Eve and challenged God's Word. Once he had her attention, it was easy to deceive her into disobeying God's command to not eat of the forbidden fruit.

I will never stop to look at what is forbidden for a minute! I will never hesitate and listen to the voice of temptation even for a second! I remember the saying, "If you let the devil ride, he will end up driving."

God's Word is truth and when Eve strayed from the truth and listened to the devil, she and Adam, along with their descendants including the entire planet, were cursed. They came out from under God's protection and blessing by their own foolish choice.

2. My "loins" are protected by God's armor—I keep my female reproductive parts pure. I am watchful not to get in any situation that would set me up for a seduction and commit fornication. I am very careful not to dress in a way that will be a temptation and a snare to men.

The Womb of Life

The womb is where new life is conceived and carried until fully developed. Thereafter the child is delivered to fulfill its destiny. We also have spiritual wombs, where God plants seeds of dreams, visions and assignments. It takes time for the seeds to grow and develop to maturity. In due season the spiritual child will be delivered. (Further explanation will be set forth in Chapter 11, "The Past is in the Tomb and the Future is in Your Womb, p. 203).

3. All of the organs and parts of my lower torso are healthy and strong. I will never suffer from barrenness because the "fruit of the womb is His reward" (Psalm 127:3)—The children that

God gives me are His blessing. It is His desire for my husband and me to produce godly seed (Malachi 2:15). He said for us to be "fruitful and multiply" (Genesis 1:28).

Single women have the privilege along with their married sisters, of conceiving in their spiritual wombs and bringing forth good fruit in their lives. Sometimes holy women birth souls into the Kingdom of God through intercession, prayer and sharing the Gospel.

SHODDING MY FEET WITH THE PREPARATION OF THE GOSPEL OF PEACE
~Ephesians 6:15~

"Shodding" is a New Testament word in the King James version meaning to "put on." When we shod our feet, we put on our spiritual fighting boots. In Bible days, the boots of the Roman soldier began just under his knee and covered his shins, calves, ankles and feet. The material over the calves was usually metal (called the "greaves"), and the covering for the feet was of strong leather studded with metal spikes. In addition, two sharp spikes protruded from the front of the boot.

The greaves protected the calves while marching through rough territory with many obstacles. They also protected the soldier from an enemy's attempts to kick his shins or break his legs. The boots provided him with secure footing. And imagine what a swift kick with the spiked boot would do to an attacker!

The Christ Woman possesses peace in the midst of any battle or storm of life, because her confidence and trust is in the "Prince of Peace."

How to Put My Gospel Boots On *(Confessions)*

1. My feet are like "hind's feet" and take me to high places (Psalm 18:30-33)—The sure-footed mountain goat (hind) is blessed with feet which allow the goat to go places where a person could never climb without falling. My footing is strong and stable when I know God's promises for my life. He always calls me to higher ground as I grow in my relationship with Him. God's boots put the supernatural on my natural feet! With Him, I will go strongly and securely where I could never have gone before.

2. Wherever my feet go, they take with them the Good News of God's salvation in Jesus Christ—No day is a "regular" day, but all days have purpose and meaning for the Christ Woman. When I get up in the morning, I sit at the feet of Jesus. I carefully listen for His Voice through the Word and the Spirit. *"If we live in the Spirit, let us also walk in the Spirit" (Galatians 5:18).* Watchman Nee taught: "Who, then is he who follows the Spirit? One who sets his mind on the things of the Spirit." When I complete my morning prayer time, I go forth seeking opportunities to minister Christ. Opportunities present themselves through my family, neighbors, co-workers, friends and everyone with whom I come into contact throughout the day. There are also planned times when I go forth to minister God's Word at a designated place and time.

3. The enemy is under my feet—Today's Christian woman may wear the latest fashionable high heels—but spiritually speaking, she can put the devil right under her feet! I am God's warrior woman and know who I am in Christ. I am well able to put my feminine foot right on the neck of the enemy! (See Joshua 10:24). I might even decide to grind my pretty, spiked heel right through his neck and nail him to the ground!

4.   My feet are protected from hurt and harm—Psalm 91 is a wonderful passage of Scripture that assures me of God's safeguard at all times and all ways. He promises to give His angels charge over me *"lest I dash my foot against a stone" (v. 12).*

PICKING UP
THE SHIELD OF FAITH
~Ephesians 6:16~

The Roman soldier had to take up his shield. That meant for it to be effective, he had to consciously pick it up, strap it to his arm and hold it in a defensive manner. It is the same way with our faith. We cannot wait for it to just happen when we need it but must be prepared at all times to defend ourselves from every attack of the enemy.

Simply put, faith is NOW. Hope is future. Faith comes from hearing the Word of God and storing it in our hearts (Romans 10:17). God's Word on the inside of us gives us total assurance that every attack of the enemy is destined for defeat in Jesus' Name. Fear is the exact opposite of faith. Fear says that God's Word is not true. There are 365 references to not fearing in the Word of God. Is it a coincidence that we receive this command once for every day of the year? Fear paralyzes the operation of God's power in our lives and opens the door for the enemy to attack us. Job lamented, *"For the thing I greatly feared has come upon me, and what I dreaded has happened to me"* (3:25).

Faith says, I believe God's Word and *"all His promises are yea and amen"* (2 Corinthians 1:20).

How to Use My Shield (Confessions)

1. I keep my shield shiny and well maintained—Every day, I study the Bible and pray. This keeps my shield radiant and strong. The sun of God's glory reflects off of my shield and blinds the eyes of the enemy!

2. I do not run from the enemy, but hold my shield up before him—To run in retreat is not an option. To stand defenseless is not smart. I am only vulnerable when I do not know and apply the Word of God to my life.

3. God's favor surrounds me as a

shield—Because I am righteous in His sight, He keeps me safe from all the wiles of the devil with *His shield* (Psalm 5:12).

I am alert at all times. When the enemy tries to throw fiery darts of anger, rejection, offence, doubt, fear, anxiety, depression or hopelessness against me, they fall off and do not penetrate. I boldly and confidently speak out loud the promises of God.

"Yet in all these things we are more than conquerors through Him who loves us" (Romans 8:37).

THE SWORD OF THE SPIRIT
~Ephesians 6:17~

We might be women but we have power that no demon can stop! Some people may think we are weak, but the Bible proclaims that we all triumph in Christ (2 Corinthians 2:14).

Glory to God, Jehovah-Tsaba, the Captain of the Lord's Hosts, has put a sword in our hand and taught us how to use it!

"For the word of God is living and powerful, and sharper than any two-edged sword…" (Hebrews 4:12).

The sword is the Word of God and when spoken with faith and authority by the Christ Woman, it becomes a mighty instrument of victory.

"Let the saints be joyful in glory, let them sing aloud on their beds. Let the high praises of God be in their mouth, and a two-edged sword in their hand, to execute vengeance on the nations, and punishments on the peoples; to bind their kings with chains and their nobles with fetters of iron; to execute on them the written judgment—this honor have all of His saints. Praise the Lord!" (Psalm 149:5-9).

Praise and worship sharpens our sword and gives us power to execute judgment on the demons who would bind people with chains and fetters. With our sword, we forcibly take those instruments and bind the adversary with them!

When Jesus fasted and prayed in the desert for 40 days and nights, satan came and tempted him three separate times. On each occasion, Jesus rebuked him with the Word of God, and each time the enemy fled before His face! Jesus was giving us an example of how to conquer the enemy of our soul.

As a soldier of Jesus Christ, you must make it your passion to know the Word of God thoroughly. Then use it well!

How to Wield the Sword of the Spirit (*Confessions*)

1. I have the power of God with His Word in my hand—Isaiah 59:19 promises that when *"the enemy comes in like a flood, the Spirit of God will hold up a standard against him."* The standard represents all of the power of the Godhead. The standard is the sword of the Lord.

In Judges 7, a judge of Israel named Gideon faced an overwhelming army of over 135,000 Midianites with his small army of only 300 men of valor. When it was time to charge, the army of Gideon shouted, *"The sword of the Lord and Gideon!"* With the Spirit of God and Gideon's leadership, the enemy turned against itself and couldn't run away fast enough! As an added bonus, in their haste they left behind all of their money and possessions.

If the sword of the Lord enabled 300 men to defeat 135,000 Midianites without a fight, how much more can God do with me—a woman who knows her authority in Christ and isn't afraid to use it!

2. With the sword of the Lord, I take back whatever the enemy has stolen from me—Now that I know who I am in

Christ, not only can I advance against the enemy and defeat him, but I can take back what he has stolen from me in the past. This is a powerful revelation. In 1 Samuel 30:17-18, I read the story of how David and his mighty men came back from war and found that the Amalakites had stolen their wives and possessions. At first David and his men were overwhelmed with grief and despair. Then David remembered the Lord his God and encouraged himself in prayer.

That's what I have to do when it looks like the enemy has succeeded in stealing from me. I have to speak God's Word and refuse to accept defeat. David sought the Lord and was instructed to go after the enemy and take back what belonged to him. The troops were rallied and took up their swords. Their courage and faith returned and they charged! They did, indeed, recover their families and possessions. *"For by You I can run against a troop, by my God I can leap over a wall" (Psalm 18:29).*

~5~
Holy Sexuality Is Powerful

"The fact that I am a woman does not make me a different kind of Christian, but the fact that I am a Christian does make me a different kind of woman."
~Elisabeth Elliot~

Sexuality, simply defined, is the innate quality a woman possesses which lets everyone know immediately that she is female. This is achieved by the way she looks, dresses, carries herself and relates with others.

Worldly sexuality can primarily be driven by unholy lust and a desire to gain self satisfaction and/or power when successfully arousing sexual desire in anyone other than one's spouse. What is lust? The word *lust* in the New Testament comes from the Greek word, *epithumia* (Strong's # 1939) which means: "...Gratifying sensual cravings, desiring the forbidden, longing for the evil, and striving for things, persons, or experiences contrary to the Word of God."

Christian sexuality is powerful because it is controlled by a desire to honor Christ in thought, appearance and behavior. It does not give place to the devil. It is not in bondage to the law (rules and regulations) but is motivated by a holy heart. A Christian woman carefully presents herself as being totally female without appealing to the carnal desires of others.

There is so much emphasis on sex in our society. What was created by God to be a beautiful expression of love between a married man and woman has been exploited, perverted, desecrated, manipulated and corrupted by satan. Temptation is everywhere; and regrettably, God's men and women are ensnared, polluted and damaged far too often. Satan beguiles them today just like he did in the garden 6,000 years ago. He gloats whenever he takes down God's people. Their failures are displayed with delight publicly for the world to see and mock. Holy witness is destroyed.

God created sex so men and women could produce godly children. Scriptures make it clear that He also wants a married man and woman to enjoy their sexuality to the full. When the Old Testament law was given, a young married man was commanded to stay with his wife for a full year without going to war so he could *"bring happiness to his wife whom he had taken" (Deuteronomy 24:5).*

Even though the Apostle Paul never married, he wrote that *"the marriage bed is undefiled."* He explained that the husband and wife have authority over one another's bodies, and they should never deny one another's needs—unless it is for an agreed-upon time of mutual prayer and fasting (1 Corinthians 7:2-5).

Christ Women can be beautiful, feminine, stylish and becoming without dressing in a seductive way. A Christ Woman does not have to dress like her grandmother, but she should always be modest—carefully avoiding tight and revealing clothing and any hint of sensuality that would excite the flesh.

"For this is the will of God, that you should be consecrated—separated and set apart for pure and holy living: that you should abstain and shrink from all sexual vice; that each of you should know how to possess [control, manage] his own body (in purity separated from things profane and) in **consecration** *and* **honor**..." *(1 Thessalonians 4:3 AMP).*

This older woman will tell the younger woman: *Keep your mysteries for your husband alone.* Some women have told me their husbands want them to dress suggestively in public "because I am proud of you." A godly, mature man of God will not want to exploit his wife in this manner. He will desire to protect her from lustful eyes. This is one time that a woman should not agree to honor her husband's wishes, because they are contrary to the Word of God. She should plainly and lovingly tell him so. Some people call this "old fashioned." The Word of God calls it "being holy."

If you are a woman who desires to be used in the ministry, let me assure you that no man—or woman—will ever respect you if you dress in a carnal manner. Men may think that you are very attractive and desirable, but they will not take you seriously as a minister of Jesus Christ.

Wolves in Sheep's Clothing

" 'Will you walk into my parlour?'
Said the Spider to the Fly,
'Tis the prettiest little
Parlour that ever you did spy;
The way into my parlour
Is up a winding stair,

And I've a many curious things to shew
When you are there.'
'Oh no, no,' said the little Fly,
'To ask me is in vain,
For who goes up your winding stair
Can ne'er come down again.'"
~Mary Howitt~

It is lamentable that we have to bring up this subject but to be "forewarned is to be forearmed." We all know that sexual harassment problems exist in the work place. But, unfortunately, there are occasionally incidents regarding sexual misconduct in the ministry. Many women are caught off guard. When God places them in a ministry, they look up to their brothers in Christ. Women expect "men of the cloth" to protect, encourage and respect them. Most of the time, this is the case. But there are predators who lurk in the shadows. The Bible calls them *"wolves in sheep's clothing."*

"Beware of false prophets, who come to you in sheep's clothing, but inwardly they are ravenous wolves" (Matthew 7:15). In this same chapter, The Message version warns, *"Don't be impressed with charisma; look for character."* Don't be caught in the trap!

Following are some clues to recognize the wolf in sheep's clothing when he begins to make his moves.

5 Typical Steps Taken In "The Hunt"

1. He starts giving attention and flattery—Honest praise for a job well done is encouraging and totally proper. However, there is a line that should never be crossed. On the other side of the line, godly appreciation turns into carnal compliments with a hidden agenda. At first a woman may feel elated with getting attention from a man she respects and admires and does not recognize the underlying intent.

2. He gradually progresses to very personal compliments and perhaps a touch here and there—Of course, all this occurs when no one else is around. A woman may begin to feel uncomfortable and not be sure how to handle this kind of attention from a minister—who is probably married and doesn't seem to care whether she is or not.

3. He will progressively become more and more familiar—He will begin sharing his personal life and a common line might be: "My wife doesn't understand the ministry like you do."

4. He will seek to get his victim alone in an office—Take heed Christ Woman. A godly man will always be prudent. Do not ever allow yourself behind a closed door with any man.

5. He will seek to get his victim alone and away from the office—This is one of the last steps of a man with improper intentions to get a woman in a vulnerable position.

5 Safeguards For Avoiding Entrapment

1. Preset boundaries—There are good Christian books on this topic, but here are a couple of tried and true safeguards:

- Always make certain there are others present. Even when intentions are honorable, we must avoid a questionable appearance.

- Whether conversing or working on a project together, we must maintain sufficient space between ourselves and a man.

2. Do not tolerate inappropriate compliments—At the first hint of these kinds of remarks, we must let the perpetrator know beyond a shadow of a doubt that it is unacceptable. A woman should tell her husband and possibly a mature Christian woman what has happened.

If comments and unsuitable attention continue, it must be clearly stated that she will not tolerate such disrespect. If the predator persists to ignore her wishes, she must get help. She MUST TELL.

3. A woman should not try to handle this alone—At this point, it is likely that she does not want to cause trouble and possibly jeopardize her position as well as his; but disclosure is absolutely necessary, otherwise her credibility could be challenged. Every incident should be fully documented in detail and recorded. The Word of God gives us good instruction in this difficult situation:

*"...You shouldn't act as if everything is just fine when a friend who claims to be a Christian is promiscuous or crooked, is flip with God, or rude to friends, gets drunk or becomes greedy and **predatory**. You can't just go along with this, treating it as acceptable behavior"* (1 Corinthians 5:9-13 The Message).

4. Stay professional in the office and discreet wherever you are at all times—As women seeking to honor and represent Christ, shouldn't we always be conservative in dress and deportment? It is never under any circumstances acceptable for a minister or any man to ever make unwelcome comments or overtures. A Christ Woman takes precautions and never puts a snare in the pathway of her brothers. Some men are strong. Others may be weak. Prudence advises women to treat all men as weak.

"Then let us...decide never to put a stumbling block or hindrance in the way of a brother" (Romans 14:13 RSV).

5. Guard your heart—If a married woman finds herself thinking about a married man more than she should or if she realizes she is dressing to please a man other than her husband, the Holy Spirit will warn her—and she better take heed.

6 Ways to Heal From A Past Entrapment

1. The "accuser of the brethren" will try to torment the woman who was a victim—A spiritual leader or brother in Christ should protect—not abuse. She was a *victim*. The accuser (satan) will condemn her and try to overwhelm her with guilt and shame. Recognize the enemy and do not entertain his accusations.

2. If the hunter lost his position, family, etc., she should not feel guilty or responsible—He brought it on himself and other women must be protected.

3. If she freely allowed herself to be used, she must confess her part to God and receive His forgiveness—and forgive herself—Most women feel victimized and were uncomfortable and troubled by the entire episode. There are some women who realized what was happening but enjoyed the relationship for a season. Eventually, both types of women want to be free from the trap and seek help from God. Our loving Father always forgives those who are sorry for their sins, and He keeps no record of wrongs. He does not want His daughters to be tormented by past failures that are covered by the Blood of Jesus.

4. She must forgive the man who took advantage of her—As difficult as it may be, she is commanded to forgive the one who sinned against her. She cannot allow herself to judge all clergy's or other men's intentions in the future because of a past painful experience.

5. If a soul tie developed (emotional bond), it must be broken and renounced—This woman must pray and ask God to help her forget and get over what happened. It probably took time to develop the soul tie, and it may take time to be totally free. She must be persistent remembering Philippians 4:13: *"I can do all things through Christ who strengthens me."*

6. Move on—The woman who was caught in the trap has learned from her experience and can rejoice in the love and restoration of God. She can proceed with her life in peace and victory in Jesus' Name.

"There is, therefore, no condemnation to those who walk according to the spirit and not according to the flesh" (Romans 8:1).

Knights In Shining White Armor

For every wolf, there are a great multitude of fine, godly men who respect women and do everything possible to support, encourage and guard their honor. They appreciate our womanhood just as we respect and are thankful for their manhood. We recognize and are blessed by the giftings and strengths of one another. Not only do they honor us, but we esteem them highly in the Lord. They are totally men, and we are totally women. As we labor together in God's holy work, we are strong in the Lord and the power of His might.

"Charm is deceitful and beauty is vain, but a woman who fears the Lord, she shall be praised" (Proverbs 31:30).

Other Seductions and Improprieties

All sexual sin is grievous. This includes fornication (Greek root words *porneia* and *pornos*—surrendering of sexual purity, promiscuity of every type, including pornography and incest— Strong's # 4202, 4205), adultery and homosexuality. The Apostle Paul explained that all other sins are committed by ourselves alone; but when we are immoral with another—male or female— we become one in the flesh with them.

"Do you not know that your bodies are members of Christ? Shall I take the members of Christ and make them members of a harlot? Or do you not know that he who is joined to a harlot is one body with her? **For 'the two' He says, 'will become**

one flesh.' *But he who is joined to the Lord is one spirit with Him.* *Flee sexual immorality.* *Every sin that a man does is outside the body, but* **he who commits sexual immorality sins against his own body"** *(1 Corinthians 6:15-28).*

Be aware that just as there are men waiting to seduce you, there are also women who lust after other women. You must be on guard against this temptation. Most women think they would never fall prey to another woman. They are in the same category as women who thought they would never commit adultery—but did.

Strong seducing spirits seek to defile men and women made in the image of God. They may seek entrance into an unsuspecting woman when her defenses are down due to disappointments or difficult problems. They prey on women who feel unloved and insecure. Temptation may also occur when anyone—male or female—gets into the wrong environment at the wrong time and is all alone.

A woman, seeking your counsel or friendship, who continually talks about sexual fantasies, weaknesses and encounters—and is not repentant and seeking deliverance—should be a red flag for you. A spiritually-sensitive Christ Woman will immediately sense the unclean spirit—in any vessel and draw away from it. The same precautions that are set forth in guarding yourself against men with lustful intentions apply to women as well.

"Behold, I sent you out as sheep in the midst of wolves. Therefore, be wise as serpents and harmless as doves" (Matthew 10:16).

Jezebel

It should be mentioned that there are some women who covet the ministry but have not overcome unholy desires that still burn within. They seek position in a church or ministry—and they also covet and lust after the man or woman of God. They are indeed a living example of *"whitewashed tombs which indeed appear beautiful outwardly, but inside are full of dead men's bones and all uncleanness" (Matthew 23:27).*

If a reader knows in her heart that she falls into this category, repent now or face a future full of regret and consequences you will not want to pay. If you are a woman who puts on a religious "show" but longs for sexual attention and thrives on stirring another's desire for you, if you are a she-wolf, read the Word of God concerning your fate:

"Nevertheless, I have a few things against you, because you allow that woman Jezebel, who calls herself a prophetess to teach and seduce My servants to commit sexual immorality...I gave her space to repent of her sexual immorality, and she did not repent. Indeed I will cast her into a sickbed, and those who commit adultery with her into great tribulation, unless they repent of their deeds. I will kill her children with death, and all the churches shall know that I am He who searches the minds and hearts And I will give to each one of you according to your works" (Revelation 2:20-23).

Integrity

The author would like to take this opportunity to add that a godly married woman will never discuss the private sexual life of her and her husband with others—male or female. She would not want her husband disclosing private information to others; and she should respect the sanctity of her marriage as well.

If a woman is having problems with her husband regarding their sexual relationship, she should seek the counsel of a mature, married Christian woman— *not a man and not even her male pastor or other minister or counselor* (unless his wife is present).

Also, as a female minister, *never* counsel with a man about sexual problems he is experiencing or any other problem unless your husband is present. If this should take place, your husband should lead the counseling session. *Men should counsel with men; women should counsel with women.*

The single woman and the married woman have consecrated their sexuality to God. Their first priority is to please Him in every aspect of their lives. A godly woman's prayer is to always give glory to God and never bring reproach to Jesus or grieve the Holy Spirit.

Holy sexuality means women are admired and respected as the King's daughters. They inspire other women to carry themselves with honor and dignity. It also means that the married woman is very desirable to her husband. Her secrets are known by him alone.

They share and enjoy every aspect of marriage with intimacy, excitement and totally satisfying love.

The author has purposely not written about sexual harassment in the work-place. There are many federal, state and municipal laws covering this complex subject.

If a reader faces a problem, she may use some of the suggestions heretofore mentioned as to the documentation of sexual abuse; but it would be prudent to seek legal advice from an attorney who specializes in this area of law.

~6~
Marriage and The Family

"At the end of the day, your relationship with your mate is only as good as your relationship with God. He is the bridge between the two of your lives."
~Michelle McKinney Mammond~

After our first priority to God and His Son Jesus Christ, our next priorities are to our husband, children and the family unit. Some women, in their zeal for advancing the Kingdom of God, neglect their husbands, children and homes. This is not God's way of doing things. We must understand God's priorities and make them our own. Whenever we rearrange priorities to suit our desires, problems inevitably follow.

In the opening pages of Genesis, God instituted marriage. As a matter of fact, he established marriage before the church.

"And the Lord God caused a deep sleep to fall on Adam, and he slept; and

He took one of his ribs, and closed up the flesh in its place. Then the rib which the Lord God had taken from man He made into a woman and He brought her to the man. And Adam said: 'This is now bone of my bones and flesh of my flesh; she shall be called Woman, because she was taken out of Man.' Therefore a man shall leave his father and mother, and be joined to his wife, and they shall become one flesh" (Genesis 2:21-24).

Marriage is holy before God, so much so that Scripture reveals that   marriage between a man and a woman is a type of Christ and His Church.

"Wives, submit to your own husbands, as to the Lord. For the husband is head of the wife, as also Christ is head of the church; and He is the Savior of the body...Husbands, love your wives, just as Christ also loved the church and gave Himself for her...This is a great mystery; but I speak concerning Christ and the church" (Ephesians 5:22, 23, 25, 32).

Many women are passionate to proclaim and advance the Gospel, and this is praiseworthy. Let's look at how women in the Bible with God's call on their lives kept their priorities in order.

Lydia was a Jewish homemaker and businesswoman. When the Apostle Paul arrived at the riverbank where she and other women were praying on the Sabbath, Lydia heard the Gospel explained for the first time. How her heart must have leapt with joy and gladness! She could not wait to go home and tell her family the good news that the Messiah had come and provided salvation for all who would believe in His Name (see Acts 16).

Her family was her first concern and the first ones she wanted to see born again. They must have received her word with gladness, because they were all saved and baptized.

There are numerous Scriptures regarding the sacredness and priority of the family. In Joshua 24:15, Joshua stood before the great camp of Israel and proclaimed, *"...But as for me and my house, we shall serve the Lord."*

Husbands

The right husband is a gift from the Lord. When a man and woman pray about their future mate and are careful to wait for God's choice, their marriage will be blessed indeed! There are many happy couples who have sound, enjoyable and fulfilling relationships. They are also excited about serving the Lord together in church, their community and other places He may lead them.

No matter how good a marriage, there will always be challenges in life. Issues arise with parents, children, finances, health and other areas. But as couples seek God, pray and defer to one another, their marriages will mature, strengthen and become more secure and satisfying as the days and years go by.

Always remember it pleases the Lord to honor your husband just as you would honor Him. Sometime, after marriage, wives see their husbands in a different light and become disappointed, critical, contemptuous and even bitter toward them. If this happens in your marriage, remember that while you are observing his supposed shortcomings, he is also seeing weaknesses and imperfections in you. Put your husband back in his rightful place.

Sometimes, Christian women marry men who are not believers. They think that after marriage they will be able to win their husbands to Christ. First of all, as Christian women, we should never marry an unbeliever because the Bible clearly warns us not to be unequally yoked. But what if a woman finds herself in that situation—the vows have already been taken and the husband is quite content to stay just the way he is?

Also, there is the situation when a woman accepts Christ after marriage and her husband is not interested in joining her in the faith. What should she do?

When Christian Women Are Married to Unbelievers

Your husband will never come to Christ through nagging, crying, preaching to him, or pleading. If he eventually comes to Christ, it will be because he sees a change in you that impresses him. Pray for God to give you great wisdom, grace and patience and follow biblical principles to show your husband the Jesus in you.

9 Tips for a Happy Marriage

1. Respect your husband—In the beginning God created man to be the provider and protector of his wife and children. He is encouraged in his role by respect from his wife. Never belittle or put your husband down. That will reveal pride in your life and turn your husband off. A woman's respect for her husband will almost always arouse tender feelings of love in his heart toward her.

2. Admire your husband—Not many

things will make a husband more happy than receiving admiration from his wife. Do you notice, appreciate and sincerely compliment your husband on a regular basis? Some women refuse to do so saying that their husbands don't deserve it and already have an inflated ego. These women again are displaying their own ego and perhaps stubbornness.

When a woman admires and appreciates her husband, his love for her grows—and he will be drawn to "what she has."

Always be genuine in your admiration. Thank your husband often for all he has done that is right and honorable.

"In like manner you married women be submissive to your own husbands— [subordinate yourselves as being secondary to and dependent on them, and adapt yourselves to them], so that even if any do not obey the Word [of God], they may be won over not by discussion but by the [godly] lives of their wives when they observe the pure and modest way in which you conduct yourselves, together with your reverence [for your husband. That is you are to feel for him all that reverence includes] - to respect, defer to, revere him; [revere means] to honor, esteem (appreciate, prize), and [in the human sense] adore him; [and adore

means] to admire praise, be devoted to, deeply love and enjoy [your husband]" (1 Peter 3:1-2 AMP).

Years ago, I taught a class for women in my church and shared these same principles. One woman in the class had been unhappily married for over twenty years. Her husband was a good provider but had a drinking problem.

She came back to our class the next week literally glowing with happiness and began to tell her story. Jennifer prayed and asked the Lord to help her with John (not their real names) in a totally different way than she had tried in the past (all unsuccessfully). The first miracle that occurred was Jennifer's attitude changed.

Jennifer prepared a good meal for her husband. After dinner, while they were relaxing and talking about the day's events, Jennifer quietly said, "John, I need to tell you something."

He braced himself for the usual barrage of complaints and condemnation over his drinking. In a soft and respectful tone, she continued, "John, in all of this time we have been married, I've never told you some things that have been in my heart. I really am thankful and appreciate all of the years that you have worked so hard to provide for our family. You have labored long hours many times and came home tired and exhausted. You have given us a beautiful home and everything we need...and John, you've always been faithful to me. I really do love you."

As Jennifer talked, John grew very quiet and listened to her intently, almost in unbelief. She had never talked to him like that before. Tears began to stream down his cheeks.

"I always thought you didn't really love me and never cared about how I felt or what I've done," John replied.

She began gently telling John all of the ways she admired and appreciated him. "John, I've been so wrong never to tell you these things before."

She told us how John then put his head down in his hands and began to weep. Her heart melted, and Jennifer fell in love with John all over again. Then, another miracle happened. John slid back in his chair, stood up and went into the room where he kept his bottles of liquor and brought them into the kitchen. While Jennifer watched, he poured all of the whiskey down the drain. Without a word, he walked to the other side of the kitchen and threw the empty bottles in the trash.

"And he hasn't had another drink all

week!" Jennifer exclaimed.

"It's been the best week of our marriage. And, he promised to attend church with me on Sunday!"

The last I heard, Jennifer and John were still doing well and he had not returned to his old habit. Not all stories end this well so quickly. The moral of the story is clear: respect, admiration and love get far more accomplished than scolding and complaining.

3. Come to an agreement on home management and responsibilities, budget, child raising, relationships with in-laws, social life, church attendance and other commitments—This should ideally be done *before marriage to avoid misunderstands and future problems.* Once your basic guidelines are established, stick to them. When adjustments are necessary from time to time, make certain you are in mutual agreement. Remember sometimes it is necessary to give and take to avoid dissention and have peace.

4. Spend quality time together—To keep your romance alive and sparkling, arrange special times together and agree to not discuss issues but just enjoy one another's company. If you have young children at home, maybe you can trade babysitting time with another couple.

If your finances are limited, be creative. There are many things to do on a very limited budget.

5. Keep up your appearance and manners—Part of the joy of dating was trying to look your best for the love of your life. You also were always courteous and thoughtful. Nothing turns off a spouse more than an unkempt appearance and inconsiderate words and attitudes. Don't forget to say "please" and "thank you."

6. Never hide anything from your spouse—Hiding something from your spouse is the same as lying. Remember that roaches hide in the dark and so does sin. Always be honest with one another.

7. Make an agreement to never raise your voices in anger, speak hateful words to one another or ever mention the word "divorce"—This is a decision that should be made *before the wedding* and any disagreements that may occur. Work together for mutual respect and harmony.

8. Study good marriage—Today, many couples marry without having had the advantage of good role models in their parents. They do not know how to treat their spouse. Purchase good books on how to have a happy marriage and study them together.

9. Pray together—The Bible is clear. There is great power when two agree in prayer. It is impossible for a couple to be in strife when they have a healthy, mutual prayer life.

Children

Children are the heritage of the Lord and "the fruit of the womb is His reward" (Psalm 127:3).

There is nothing like the wonder of pregnancy. A tiny child is created at the moment of conception and immediately begins to develop and grow. When we know that a child is buried deep within our womb, we feel special in a way only a woman can understand. All through the pregnancy, we take unusual care of ourselves, pray for our baby and make plans. Our husbands carefully watch over us to make sure we don't hurt ourselves or have unnecessary strain. As soon as the little one begins to kick and make its presence known, we are amazed and lovingly place our hands on our tummies further connecting with our baby.

It's difficult to comprehend why so many women don't want their child and end the tiny life before it ever has a chance to come into the world. It is highly probable that some dear woman at this moment is regretting an abortion she endured in the past.

Perhaps, she was young and scared or someone else demanded or talked her into it. Now, she is sorry and regrets her choice and has asked God's forgiveness over and over again. If you are such a woman, even though abortion is a grave sin, God forgives if you ask Him out of a sincere and repentant heart; your baby is in heaven waiting to have a glorious reunion with you someday.

Once children are born, some women are so exuberant about their children that they put them before their husbands because of a strong desire to be the absolutely best mother possible. This is a serious mistake some women unknowingly make. Review your priorities on a regular basis to avoid problems.

We are responsible, together with our husbands, to raise our children in the fear and admonition of the Lord. We are supposed to love, train, care for and encourage our children in every way possible—but not at the expense of our marriage. By having a close and strong relationship with our husbands, our children will not feel second class but will be happy and secure in their loving and stable home—and will most likely follow their parents' example after they start their own families.

Today, our children are being bombarded with every temptation imaginable and unimaginable. They are often confused about their beliefs, sexuality and the meaning of life. Many are fearful, depressed, discouraged and insecure. They excessively pierce, tattoo, cut themselves and dress strangely to attract attention and make a personal statement to fit in with the crowd.

Too often children are addicted to alcohol, drugs, porn, violent and occult video games, sex and more. They are angry, defiant and looking for a place to implode or explode.

This is not just happening in "the world," it is happening in the church. What can we do to protect our families and ensure confidence and security? How can we help them to know God loves them and He is real?

10 Tips for Raising Children

1. Establish a family altar (Deuteronomy 6:6-9)— A family *altar* will *alter* your family! A family altar is simply making time every day to come together as a family and have a devotion.

There is an old saying that is really true, "The family that prays together will stay together."

2. Establish divine order in the home, and you will have peace in the home (1 Timothy 3:4)— The dad is the spiritual head of the home. The man leads with strength, authority and love. Ideally, he and his wife have a mutual respect and administrate their home together. Children *never* dictate the rule of the home. They are raised to honor and submit to their parents' authority.

Ephesians 6:2 gives clear instructions: *"Honor your father and mother, which is the first commandment with promise: that it may be well with you and you may live long on the earth."*

I have counseled many women who have wept over their older children— preteen through young adult—not respecting them or their husbands. My heart goes out to them. Here is the plain truth: It is difficult (but not impossible with God's help) to get a child's rebellious, defiant and disrespectful attitude to change once they reach a certain age. The time to set the standard for order in the home is the day the baby is brought home from the hospital.

3. Predetermine and set rules for the

children and be consistent in applying them (Matthew 18:19)— Parents should carefully and prayerfully predetermine the rules of the home and always stand together in enforcing them. Do not keep changing your mind. Never allow children to play you and their father against one another. You must have a united front to be effective in your parenting.

4. Support one another and do not disagree in front of the children (Matthew 12:25)— Jesus taught that a house divided against itself will not stand. When parents support one another and are consistent with their rules and discipline, children will not be inclined to argue.

5. Apply loving discipline when appropriate (Proverbs 13:24)— When a child willfully breaks rules or displays inappropriate behavior, action must be taken according to the predetermined punishment that the parents have decided upon. Firmly explain to the child why they are being corrected and administer punishment. When the child is quiet, explain there are consequences for breaking rules. Then reassure the child of your love and care.

6. Do not criticize church or any authorities (Titus 3:2)— Of course, parents should not be critical of anyone whether they are in front of their children or not. When a parent does criticize authority, the children will learn not to respect authority—and that includes YOU!

7. Guard your mouth and only speak LIFE to your children—and one another (Proverbs 18:21)—Be lavish in the praise and affirmation of your children. When you do correct your children, be careful not to tear them down personally with words like, "You are dumb!" or "You are bad!" You might say, "What you *did* was dumb—you are much smarter than that!" Or you could say, "What you *did* was not right!" Choose your words care-fully.

8. Attend church regularly with your children (Hebrews 10:25)—Always take your children with you to church on a weekly basis. This will engrain in them at an early age how important it is to honor the House of God. Also, they will learn about worship, prayer and principles from the Word of God. They will be blessed by the added security of their pastor and other spiritual leaders. Our children made friends in the church nursery, attended grade school and high school with many of them and have kept their friendships to this day.

9. Live with integrity before your children (1 Peter 5:3)— It's praiseworthy to diligently teach your children the ways of the Lord, but you must practice what you preach to make a lifelong effect on their lives.

10. Love and respect one another— nothing will make your children happier or more secure (John 13:34-35)— Someone said that the greatest gift a father can give his children is to love their mother. It works both ways. Women also send a powerful message to their children when they love and respect their father. Never belittle or talk negatively about your husband to the children. Instead, praise him and show honor at every opportunity.

Upon following these guidelines, children will learn early that Jesus Christ is the center of their home life. They will see your devotion to Him and learn lessons from you that no Sunday School teacher can teach as well.

Biblical Priorities
To Remember
(Ephesians 5 & 6)

1. God
2. Spouse
3. Children
4. Other

~7~
The Single Woman

*"Let me be a woman, holy through
and through, asking for nothing but
what God wants to give me..."*
~Elisabeth Elliot~

I have lived long enough to make some interesting observations. One is the majority of single women cannot wait to get married, and a great many married women want to be single again. So, it appears that until we find contentment on the inside, it is impossible to find contentment on the outside. Some women are single by choice. They feel no desire for a companion and enjoy their independence. Other women are single by choice because of their ministry. For instance, many women have served Christ as nuns. Mother Theresa is a prime example of a woman who gave her entire life to serving others.

Some women are single and feel their destiny and calling is to be completed with a husband. This calling is noble also. Whether they are called to be single or called to be married, what is important is they find God's will and live it to the best of their ability. Sometimes those who want to be married must wait. They wait because it is in their best interest to not get ahead of God's perfect timing. Perhaps He is doing a work in them or in a prospective spouse, and the work is not finished yet. So, whether a woman is single by choice or single and waiting for a husband, she should be content in the Lord.

"...For I have learned in whatever state I am, to be content: I know how to be abased, and I know how to abound. Everywhere and in all things I have learned both to be full and to be hungry, both to abound and to suffer need" *(Philippians 4:11-12).*

Single—Without Children

"But I want you to be without cares, for the things of the Lord—how (she) may please the Lord...And this I say for your own profit, not that I may put a leash on you, but for what is proper, and that you may serve the Lord without distraction" *(1 Corinthians 7:32,35—Word gender in parenthesis changed by author).*

Space does not permit recounting inspirational stories of thousands of single women who have led fulfilling and meaningful lives. One example is Amy Carmichael (1867-1951) who was one of the most famous women missionaries. For over 50 years, she labored in India providing a home for orphans and rescued many young girls from temple prostitution. She authored more than 35 books and by 1952, over 900 women had joined her fellowship, Sisters of the Common Life. At one point, while she was still young, Amy grew anxious about being lonely in life and grew concerned about her future. She went away to a cave and sought God with all of her heart.

"Lord, what can I do? How can I go on to the end?" He answered, "None of them that trust in Me shall be desolate." That word kept her all of her life.

Whether a single woman is called to be a missionary or to be a good neighbor, her life will have purpose and meaning as she lives for Christ.

Single—With Children

It is no small task to raise children

as a single mother. Sometimes women are left alone because of divorce, others are widowed, and still others have had children out of wedlock. Whatever the case, Jesus Christ is there to give strength and help.

Dr. Charles Stanley was born in 1932 and nine months later, his father died. It was tragic for his mother, Rebecca, and Charles. Rebecca raised Charles with much love and taught him about Jesus on a daily basis. Not only did she teach him, but she lived an exemplary life before her only son. For years, she worked two jobs as she struggled to raise Charles alone. Dr. Stanley tenderly re-members her many sacrifices for him and devotion to God and himself. Every night she would kneel by his bedside, and they would pray together. At the age of 12, Charles was born again and at age 14, he answered the call of ministry. Today, he has pastored a megachurch in Atlanta, Georgia, for over 50 years and his "In Touch" radio and TV program is broad-cast around the world in more than 50 languages.

Rebecca Stanley experienced deep sorrow and many challenges as a young widow with a child to raise by herself. But with a big faith in God and dedication, she raised him to fulfill his destiny in Christ.

Not every child is called to be a Charles Stanley, but every child has a destiny. If you are a single mother and ask God to help you raise your children successfully, you will not be disappointed.

A Mother's Influence

I took a piece of plastic clay
And idly fashioned it one day;
And as my fingers pressed it still,
It moved and yielded at my will.
I came again when days were past,
The form I gave it still it bore,
And as my fingers pressed it still,
I could change that form no more.
I took a piece of living clay,
And gently formed it day by day.
And molded with my power and art,
A young child's soft
And yielding heart.
I came again when days were gone;
It was a man I looked upon
He still that early impress bore,
And I could change it never more.

(This classic poem was written by an unknown author and published in the "Bible Friend.")

Your children are your greatest ministry while you have the privilege of raising them for Christ. Put your shoulders back, and take one day at a time.

"Call to Me, and I will answer you, and show you great and mighty things, which you do not know" (Jeremiah 33:3).

Senior Singles

Some dear saints of God find themselves alone in their silver years due to widowhood or other reasons. They can become very lonely and feel like their lives have no meaning or purpose.

My mother-in-law, Bernice, was a widow for over 20 years. When her husband passed away at age 68, she made up her mind not to grieve for long and to continue serving Jesus with all of her heart. She had given birth to eight children and, together with her husband, raised them to honor God and live worthy and productive lives. (One child was killed in a car accident at an early age.)

Bernice always had a smile on her face and a song in her heart. She spent her widowhood taking friends to the doctor, helping with the grandchildren, doing good deeds and serving as a volunteer at her church. Every day she met with the Lord for her time of prayer and intercession. She praised Him continually in word and deed. Her life was simple and unassuming. Bernice never sought attention or even thanks. She just loved the Lord and wanted to be a blessing

Today, I am convinced that she has a high reward in heaven—right next to men and women of renown who went on before her. Her loving spirit made a great impression on me, and I am very grateful.

Some senior singles are quite content to remain single and other dear ones decide to marry again. If both parties feel strongly attracted to one another, have prayed sincerely for God's direction and have His peace, then they should marry and enjoy the rest of their days together in the Lord. This, too, is acceptable and a blessing.

.

~8~

The Mentor and The Mentee

*"An excellent minister has
learned to receive instruction
without being offended."*
~Robb Thompson~

Dr. Daisy Washburn-Osborn (1924-1995)
and her husband, Dr. T. L. Osborn, won
millions of souls to Christ through mass
evangelism. Dynamic Daisy also blazed a
trail for women called to minister the
Gospel of Jesus Christ.

In the early nineties, I was privileged
to hear great teachings from Dr. Daisy at
a women's conference hosted by my home
church at the time, Evangel Christian
Life Center in Louisville, Kentucky. Hundreds of eager women attended the conference and had a great desire to follow
her footsteps in the ministry.

We all listened intently to every word.
I will always remember advice from the
wise woman of God. It went something

like this: "Every woman who desires to grow and flourish in Christ needs a mentor. A mentor is a woman who has gone before her in the ministry. She has plowed the fallow ground, planted seed and watered it with her tears. Through patience and persistence, together with much prayer, she has seen the green shoot come out of the ground, grow and then finally be harvested. This is a woman who can spare you much heartache and frustration. Sit at her feet and learn everything you can. Go to her for advice and prayer. Treasure her.

"By the same token, there is a young woman somewhere who needs you. You have gone ahead of her and know more about serving Christ than she has experienced. Ask God to reveal her to you. And when you know who she is, pour your love into her and teach her all that she is willing to learn. We all need a mentor and a mentee. That keeps us balanced. We are giving and receiving."

In the book of Ruth, we read the touching story of a young woman and her mother-in-law whose name was Naomi. Naomi was a Jewess and had been born in Bethlehem. She and her husband,

Elimelech, had two sons, Mahlon and Chilion. When the boys were young, a scorching famine came upon the land. People were desperate for food and sustenance. So, Elimelech decided it would be best to leave their home in Bethlehem and move to Moab which was about 30 miles away on the other side of the Dead Sea.

The family settled in Moab, which was a pagan land that worshipped the false god Chemosh and sometimes offered him human sacrifices. The founding father of the nation was Moab. Moab was born from an incestuous relationship between Lot and one of his daughters (Genesis 19). So the spiritual climate of the land was not desirable for a good Jewish family.

In the process of time, Elimelech died and Naomi was left with two sons who wanted to marry. The first chapter of Ruth tells us that the sons took for themselves Moabite wives. But their marriages did not last long because a short time thereafter, both Mahlon and Chilion died also. We are not told the circumstances of their deaths. Naomi must have been devastated after having lost not only her husband but her two sons. She changed her name to Mara meaning "bitter." Without a man to provide for her and her daughters-in-law, Naomi decided to go back home to Bethlehem and made preparations. Sadly, she called Orpah and Ruth to her side and released them:

"Go, return each to her mother's house. The Lord deal kindly with you, as you have dealt with the dead and with me. The Lord grant that you may find rest, each in the house of her husband" (Ruth 1:8-9).

Orpah reluctantly left Naomi. Ruth clung to her, not wanting to leave. She begged Naomi to take her along to Bethlehem. Naomi discouraged her, not knowing what hardships may lie ahead. Ruth passionately replied with these immortal words:

"Entreat me not to leave you, or to turn back from following after you; for wherever you go, I will go, and wherever you lodge, I will lodge; your people shall be my people, and your God, my God. Where you die, I will die, and there will I be buried. The Lord do so to me, and more also, if anything but death parts you and me" (v. 16).

Ruth had obviously learned to love Naomi very much. She had seen something in Naomi that caused her never to leave. Is it not likely that she also had met Naomi's God, Jehovah, and desired to serve Him along with Naomi? With great resolve, courage and determination, Ruth was willing to leave her land, her family, her religion, friends and everything familiar to follow Naomi. Together, they traveled back to Bethlehem.

When Naomi and Ruth entered Bethlehem, *"all the city was excited because of them."* Naomi came back home with nothing but her young daughter-in-law and little else to her name. Ruth sat at Naomi's feet and respectfully listened to her every word of advice. Ruth never questioned Naomi but did everything she said, even if it meant working long, hard days harvesting barley in the fields.

In this day and time, many people expect instantaneous results from little or no effort. Good things and answers to prayer do not always come immediately. God, in His wisdom, works with us to develop faith, character and integrity.

Ruth persevered. She obeyed. She labored. She handled herself wisely and blessed Naomi with her earnings. Her attitude and actions did not go unnoticed by Boaz the owner of the fields—the richest man in town, who turned out to be Naomi's relative.

There is a set time for God to move, and there is a set time for a blessing! Christ Woman, a godly mentor is a gift from God. She might just help you move into a field that will bless you and many others for the rest of your life! It might not look positive or pleasant at first. However, you can always have confidence that it is God's will to bless you!

"I waited patiently for the Lord; and He inclined to me, and heard my cry. He also brought me up out of a terrible pit, out of the miry clay, and set my feet upon a rock, and established my steps. He has put a new song in my mouth—praise to our God; many will see it and fear, and will trust in the Lord" (Psalm 40:1-3).

It wasn't long before Ruth married Boaz. They had a son and named him Obed. Obed was none other than the father of Jesse. Jesse was the father of King David and an ancestor of Jesus Christ.

What if Ruth had not been willing to step out in faith? What if Ruth had wanted to do things her own way and not heeded the advice of Naomi? What if she had not labored in the field and waited patiently for God to meet her at the point of her need? The answer is that she would have missed a tremendous blessing and fulfilling her destiny.

What about you? Have you been

disappointed in the past? Is your present situation discouraging and the future looking dim? Follow the example of Ruth and take a step in faith. Humble yourself and sit at the feet of a godly spiritual mother.

Then, turn around and look behind you at another upcoming young woman. Perhaps, she hasn't walked where you have walked but wants to go where you are going.

Take her by the hand.

5 Things to Know About A Mentor

1. Search for her—What is it you feel called to do for the Lord? Look for a woman who has excelled in that area and has years of experience and a good reputation. She will probably not be looking for you, so be willing to make the first move. Invest your time with her, and ask her to help you—but only if you really mean it and are willing to make the commitment.

2. She will be a spiritual mother and not a best friend—A mother has your best interest at heart and will not always tell you what you want to hear. She will

112

encourage you—and sometimes correct you. Do not be offended and receive correction graciously.

3. Spend time with her on a regular basis (Proverbs 12:20)—As with any investment, you will get out of the relationship whatever you are willing to put into it. Consider all time with her valuable. Ask her questions. Listen and learn.

4. She will be your bridge to other meaningful relationships—It has been said that everyone is only seven people away from anyone in the world. Your mentor knows people you need to meet, and they will help you grow.

5. The anointing of your mentor will transfer to you—Timothy, Titus, Barnabas and other young men had fire in their souls to accomplish the same works as Paul the Apostle. They attached themselves to him and sat at his feet. In the beginning, they were willing to serve and take the low place. But after a time of learning and passing many tests, Paul's anointing to win souls and establish churches fell on them.

5 Things to Know About A Mentee

1. She will likely approach you and ask that you mentor her—First, spend time with her, listen to her heart and observe her spirit. Then, after prayer, you can decide whether or not to make the commitment of your time and effort. If you do feel led by the Holy Spirit to take her under your wing, consider her a sacred trust.

2. Always speak the truth in love—At times, you will want to tell her what she wants to hear just to make her feel better. Never do that. Always, tell her in love what the Word of God says about her situations and challenges.

3. When she has earned your trust, provide opportunities for her (Galatians 2:1)— Once again, we look at Paul and how he mentored the young men who followed him. When the time was right, he took them to Jerusalem and introduced Titus and Timothy to the apostles and other church leaders.

When you know that she is ready, introduce your mentee to friends who can encourage and open doors for her.

114

4. Take up for her when necessary—As she begins to step out and do things she has never done before, she may receive criticism or not be understood. She may make some mistakes. When she needs you as a spiritual mentor and mother to stand up for her, do not hesitate.

5. Pray for her and ask God to anoint her for ministry—When you feel she has matured sufficiently in the Lord, lay your hands on her and pray for the Holy Spirit to impart an anointing on her for His ministry.

Here is a word of wisdom and warning: Hopefully, you will never be disappointed by your mentee whose motives have gone awry, or is not serious about developing her gifts, or is compromising her life as a Christian. If that should ever prove to be the case, prayerfully and carefully confront her. This may be difficult for you but is absolutely necessary. Yes, it would be easier to not schedule time with her anymore. However, she may benefit from a loving but firm heart-to-heart talk about the weaknesses you are observing in her life. If the mentee receives your words with a good attitude, then she will grow in Christian maturity and grace. If she does not, it is time for you to be relieved of mentoring her. Make sure you do so in peace. You can agree to disagree.

Thankfully, there will also be the rewarding times when you will joyfully watch a mentee grow in her calling and go forward toward her goals with confidence and strength. There may even come a day, when your season of ministry is drawing to a close, and you will pray for God to transfer your call and anointing to a spiritual daughter.

Moses mentored Joshua for 40 years in the desert. Just before the children of Israel were ready to cross over to the Promised Land, God told Moses that he could not go. It was Moses' time to be laid to rest. He had finished his assignment. It was time for Joshua to take his place and fulfill his personal destiny. He was prepared. He was ready and proceeded to take Israel across the Jordon to the Promised Land (Deuteronomy 34:9).

~9~
Women in Ministry

*"The church that silences women
is shorn of half its power."*
~Charles G. Finney~

What is the Ministry?

*"And he Himself gave some to be apostles,
some prophets, some evangelists and
some pastors and teachers, for the equipping of the saints for the work of the
ministry, for the edifying of the body of
Christ (Ephesians 4:11-12).*

Ministry comes from the Greek word,
diakonia, which means, "attendance (as a
servant, etc.)...service of the Christian
teacher..." (Strong's #1248). In Modern
days, many have applied the meaning to
be only vocational such as in the office of
a pastor. Ministry (serving) is a lifestyle
for *all* Christians and certainly is at the
heart of every position and vocation in
the Body of Christ.

Every calling is vital to fulfill God's
purposes—whether a person is called to

be an apostle or church janitor. Some-day, when we are judged for our works, we will be rewarded as to whether or not we successfully and faithfully completed the work Christ called us to do in His Body. The apostle and the janitor who completed their assignments with an equal "work of faith and labor of love" will be rewarded equally.

"For as the body is one and has many members, but all the members of that one body, being many, are one body, so also is Christ. For by one Spirit we were all baptized into one body—whether Jews or Greeks, whether slaves are free—and have all been made to drink into one Spirit. For in fact the body is not one member but many...

"And the eye cannot say to the hand, 'I have no need of you,' nor again the head to the feet, 'I have no need of you.' No, much rather, those members of the body which seem to be weaker are neces-sary" (1 Corinthians 12:12-14, 20-21).

We live in a day and age when women enjoy more liberty than ever before. Many denominations are now accepting women who have leadership abilities into ministry positions within the church. It is a time to take advantage of every opportunity God gives us, but we must carefully follow biblical teaching and instructions. The third chapter of Proverbs tells us that with all of our getting we should get wisdom. With the wisdom and grace of God, we as women can effectively work and minister with our brothers in Christ—and all other Christians male and female, young and elderly.

(It is very evident that the enemy does not hesitate to use anybody and everybody he can recruit to advance his purposes!)

A Woman's Place

In 1 Timothy 2:12, Paul writes, *"...I do not permit a **woman** to teach or to have authority over a **man** but to be in silence."* The Greek word, *gyne* can either be translated "woman" or "wife," and the Greek word *aner* can either be translated "man" or "husband" depending on the context. So this Scripture could mean simply that a woman does not take authority over or instruct her husband. It does not mean that *all* men have authority over *all* women. Of course, women in ministry always respect Scriptural authority (as do *all* Christians, male and female).

In some cases, the reference will be

to her husband in a joint-ministry situation. If the ministry is a position within the church, the authority will be the pastor/senior elder of the church where she is ministering. A woman minister can confidently serve in her calling, but she always graciously defers to Scriptural authority.

"Obey those who rule over you, and be submissive, for they watch out for your souls, as those who must give an account. Let them do so with joy and not with grief, for that would be unprofitable for you" *(Hebrews 13:17).*

Husband and Wife Teams

Priscilla and Aquila were a married couple and friends of the Apostle Paul. They were tentmakers by trade and established a church in their home (1Corinthians 16:19). While Priscilla and Aquila were in Ephesus and the Apostle Paul (who was also a tentmaker by trade) was in Antioch, they met Apollos *"an eloquent man and mighty in the Scriptures" (Acts 18:24).* Apollos had only been exposed to the teachings of John the Baptist, so Priscilla and Aquila took him aside and fully explained Christianity. (The Scriptures clearly say "they" instructed Apollos.) It is reasonable to conclude that Aquila initiated and led their conversations, but Priscilla was also free to interject her understanding and experience. In addition, it is important to note that Aquila and Priscilla *"took Apollos aside"* (privately) for instruction.

The Salvation Army (originally called the Christian Mission) was founded by William and Catherine Booth in 1865. Catherine (1829-1890) had a strong Christian upbringing and read the Bible through eight times before she was 12 years old. When she became a young woman, Catherine met William Booth (1829-1912) who was a Methodist minister. They shared a common call and burden to see people saved and delivered from addictions, especially alcohol. Catherine and William had great compassion for the poor and needy. After a three-year courtship, they were married and immediately started ministering together.

Catherine, affectionately and respectfully called "Army Mother," expanded the Salvation Army to include "reclaiming" women from a life of prostitution.

From the beginning of the Salvation Army, women were welcomed into service and shared equal opportunity with the brothers. As a matter of fact William Booth once stated, "My best men are women." Catherine shared the pulpit with her husband, William, and is said to have been a forceful and dynamic preacher.

The couple had eight children who all lived to adulthood (unusual in those days) and served in the Salvation Army. When William and Catherine were promoted to heaven, their children carried on their great work.

Today, many married couples serve in the ministry together. They may be church or lay ministers. When they share a passion for advancing God's Kingdom and labor together in the Gospel, their influence is greatly enhanced. Deuteronomy 32:30 states that one chases a thousand and two ten-thousand!

Another great promise comes from Matthew 18:19: *"Again I say to you that if two of you agree on earth concerning anything they ask, it will be done for them by My Father in heaven."*

Women Called to the Ministry Whose Husbands Are Not

Occasionally, the situation arises when a woman is called to the five-fold ministry of apostle, prophet, evangelist, pastor/teacher or some other service to the Lord—and her husband is not. Let's look at wisdom from God's Word about this.

When Her Husband is Not A Christian

If the woman's husband is not a Christian and does not want her to serve, it presents a very difficult challenge. This woman must continue to honor and respect her husband and pray diligently for his salvation and understanding. Whatever she does for the work of the Lord will have to be done in such a way that it does not cause her husband's resentment. This woman should be patient and do what she can within the boundaries of her marital and maternal responsibilities. Hopefully, in due season, her husband will be so impressed and pleased with her love and care for him and the home that he will eventually release her to fulfill her calling—and become a believer as well.

When Her Husband is A Christian

The best situation is when the woman has a calling to minister, and her husband supports her calling in Christ. He is secure in his relationship with Christ—and his own calling—and does not feel threatened by her endeavors and accomplishments. He is a dedicated man of God.

I know married women who have been called to preach. Their husbands are happy to go with them and support them in the ministry. This is a great comfort to the woman minister, because she knows that her husband is not only covering her spiritually but also in the natural. If anyone would attempt to cause her trouble or harm in any way, they will have to deal with her husband. The people to whom she is ministering will also feel the same security and be more accepting of her ministry knowing that her husband supports her.

She also includes her husband in the ministry by asking for him to pray, encourage and assist her when needed. This woman always defers to her husband if he should feel led to interject his comments or revelation from the Lord.

Women Pastoring Churches

This is a topic that can truly upset many Christians. It is my understanding from Scripture that it is God's plan for men to lead whenever possible. However, there are times—such as when the Prophetess and Judge, Deborah led Israel to battle (Judges 4 and 5)—that God raises up a woman to lead and prophesy. Revelation 19:10 states that the *"testimony of Jesus is the spirit of prophecy."* What is the testimony of Jesus? It is simply telling who Jesus is and what He has done and will do now and in the future according to the Word of God.

Let's take a look at a couple of New Testament examples of women leading assemblies. Remember that in the time of the early church, services were held in private homes, not in formal structures as we have today. Lydia's conversion and baptism, along with her household, has already been mentioned. Let's look a little deeper.

"Now a certain woman named Lydia heard us...the Lord opened her heart to heed the things spoken by Paul" (See

(Acts 16:14).

Obviously, Lydia was a woman of prayer, because she was praying with other women when Paul first met her. And since the Bible tells us that "she and her whole household" were saved and baptized, we assume that she had a husband and children. Perhaps, extended family members lived in her home as well. If she indeed did have a husband, he opened their home to be a gathering place for believers. He obviously approved of her work for the Lord.

In Colossians 4:15, Paul greeted Nympha who had opened her home for meetings of the brethren. If her husband were pastor, Paul would not have been so ungracious as to not greet him. It is possible, that these women were widows or had never married, but Scripture is silent on their marital state.

Actually, a church is a group of Christians gathered together to worship God, study Scriptures, receive the Lord's Supper, and pray for one another. Visitors and unbelievers are always encouraged to join the fellowship. Whether the believers are gathered together in a home, a modern church structure or a stadium, it is still a Christian assembly of *ecclesia*—"called-out ones." We call it "church."

If a woman has a word from God and the testimony of Jesus, she should by all means obey God in what He has called her to say and do—always in divine order and submitting to the church's overseeing elder.

Women Serving In The Church

We should also discuss how women should relate and work with men in the ministry. How can they avoid pitfalls and problems? This subject is personal since I have served in various roles in the church over the years. In every case, I was under the authority of the church's male pastor. I have also been in a position to observe women and men working together in a number of different capacities. Sometimes a man and woman will need to work closely together on an almost daily basis. An example may be a senior pastor and his administrative assistant; or as in my case a senior male pastor with an associate pastor who is female. The following guidelines will protect both parties and assure everyone in the church that the relationship is above reproach.

8 Guidelines for Women Ministers

1. Ideally, one woman working in close association with one man should be significantly older than he—There will be honorable exceptions, but this is a sensible safeguard against anyone ever thinking something may be unwholesome about the relationship. The spouses of both parties should be very comfortable with the working arrangement also. If one of the spouses has reservations that are not considered, there will always be resentment that their feelings were not important to his or her spouse. This may open a door for a spirit of jealousy and suspicion. A spouse's reluctance to bless the relationship may also be a warning signal. In truth God may be protecting everyone involved. If a husband's feelings are not really justified, the wife should still respect her husband enough to make different arrangements. God always honors these kinds of choices.

2. Be friendly but not overly familiar with the opposite sex—This may sound old fashioned, but many marriages would still be intact today if this wisdom were observed by everyone.

3. Be assertive and feminine at the same time (1 Samuel 25)—Many years ago at the onset of my ministry, a wise elderly woman, Helen Sandrella, said to me, "Go forward in your God-given calling with your authority in Christ. But make sure you never take on a 'man spirit.'" I have not forgotten her words. She meant that even though women may be used in positions and vocations that are typically filled by men, they should always remember that they are women. We retain our femininity in actions, demeanor, dress and our whole manner of life.

4. Think before you speak. Do not chatter (Proverbs 17:28)—Oh, let's admit it. We as women can get chatty. Talk, talk, talk. We like the details! But men usually want to keep to the main thing. When conversing with the brothers, stay focused and stick with the primary topic.

5. Do not display undue emotion ("drama") (Colossians 3:12-14,17 *The Message*)— "*So, chosen by God for this new life of love, dress in the wardrobe God picked out for you: compassion, kindness, humility, quiet strength, discipline. Be even tempered, content with second place, quick to forgive an offense. Forgive as quickly and completely as the Master forgave you. And regardless of what else you put on, wear love. It's your basic, all-purpose garment. Never be without* *it...Let every detail in your lives—words, actions, whatever—be done in the name of the Master, Jesus, thanking God the Father every step of the way."*

One outburst of anger, one demonstration of resentment, one tearful breakdown will cause a loss of respect with your peers. Those few moments of undisciplined emotion may also cost you a promotion or advancement in God's work. That's just the way it is ladies.

6. Timidity invites disdain and attack (Proverbs 29:25)—Women do not respect men who are cowardly, unkempt and lazy. Men do not respect women who whine, lack confidence and display timidity. Remember that femininity and weakness are not the same. The devil will certain take advantage of any sign of fear, insecurity or doubt on your part. Now, hold your chin up, and move forward with assurance and Christ-like dignity.

7. Do not distract (1Timothy 2:9)—Of course, we will always be modest in our attire, and we must dress appropriately for the church office or ministry meeting. Earrings swinging around, layers of bracelets clanging, strong perfume, etc. can be very distracting. It is better to err on the side of being too conservative if we want to be taken seriously and gain respect as a Christ Woman.

8. Watch out for pride and arrogance! (Proverbs 16:18)—Yes, we have faith and confidence. Yes, we know who we are in Christ. Yes, we are *"more than conquerors."* But we always remember that without Christ, we are nothing. Stay humble. Keep a servant spirit. Women or men who get full of themselves and demand service and attention are missing the entire Christian message. Those who give themselves titles and insist on recognition are not properly representing the Gospel.

Moses was one of the greatest leaders of all time. God used him to lead millions of people from bondage to freedom. Notice, the Bible says that he was *"...A very humble man, the most humble man on the face of the earth" (Numbers 12:3 NIV).*

It really only matters what God thinks of us. We should always have one desire and goal and that is to bring Him honor, glory and praise!

"And whatever you do, do it heartily, as to the Lord and not to men, knowing that from the Lord you will receive the reward of the inheritance; for you serve the Lord Jesus Christ" (Colossians 3:23-24).

~10~
Coverings, Authority And Position

*"Only one under authority
can be an authority."*
~Watchman Nee~

Currently, millions of people around the world are homeless. Even in the United States of America, thousands of destitute men, women and even children sleep in the open. At night, they are not only exposed to the elements but also to hurt and harm.

The natural covering of a home protects us from heat and cold, rain, snow and harsh winds. It gives us privacy and safety from unwanted visitors, insects and animals. It is a place of love, nurturing and comfort. God has also provided spiritual coverings for His children. They are to safeguard us and provide a place of security under His banner.

(Please note that we are *not* referring

134

to the "shepherding movement" that was popular years ago. It emphasized submission to a personal pastor/shepherd and eventually brought accusations of authoritarianism.)

Jesus Christ's atoning Blood is THE primary covering that saves and protects us from evil.

However, it is prudent and wise to understand, appreciate and honor the protection God has provided for us in regards to authority.

We will study four primary authorities: God, husband, church and government—but there are additional ones which may apply in other circumstances.

God

"You shall have no other gods before Me" (Exodus 20:3). No other power, law or mandate can overrule the law of God. His Word and His laws are the final authority and trump all other laws and authority.

When the Israelites traveled through the desert for forty years, God watched over them day and night. Moses, their appointed leader, regularly met with Him and received instructions on the way and manner he was to lead the people. After the Ten Commandments were given to Moses on Mt. Sinai, they established and defined the law of God that the people were to follow. Even if Moses, himself, had asked the people to do something in violation of God's commands—the people would have been bound to keep the laws of God before Moses.

Husband

There has been much written on this subject. The fact of the matter is that a married woman is to honor her husband before any other authority other than God (Ephesians 5:22-27).

Blessed is the woman who has a Christian husband who understands the importance of being the spiritual protector and head of the home. He loves and cherishes his wife and family. The husband watches over his wife and is careful to guard and care for her and the family.

"Even so husbands should love their wives as [being in a sense] their own bodies. He who loves his own wife loves himself. For no man ever hated his own flesh, but **nourishes** *and* **carefully protects**

and cherishes it, as Christ does the church..." (Ephesians 5:28-29 AMP).

When over-zealous women venture out on their own without the approval and support of their husbands, they come out from under the spiritual protection which God has provided for them.

Whenever we rebel against God's way of doing things, we open the door for the enemy to come in with an attack. (See 1 Samuel 15:23 *"...rebellion is as the sin of witchcraft...").* Even if a husband has not trusted Christ as his Savior, the wife is told to defer to his authority when decisions need to be made.

(The only time a wife would not honor her husband's decision would be if the husband asked her to do something against God's Word. For instance, if a husband wanted his wife to watch pornography or accompany him to ungodly environments, she is not to submit in these types of situations.)

What About Singles?

God has certainly not forgotten those who are single, divorced or widowed. Those who are single are always covered by Jesus Christ—as every Christian is covered by Christ's atonement. Single women retain the protection of their fathers while still living at home.

They also find   strength and security within their church. No Christian woman stands alone.

The church is also instructed to care for qualifying widows (1 Timothy 5:15-16) who have no family. In Isaiah 54:4, we read of how our loving God   covers the widow: *"For your Maker is your husband—the Lord Almighty is His Name— the Holy One of Israel is your Redeemer."*

The Church

The church is a very important covering for the entire family. The church and its leadership provide another umbrella of protection against the forces of evil. Jesus Christ established the church for believers to gather and worship Him, grow in knowledge of the Word, receive ministry, prayer and have fellowship with one another.   The enemy hates the church and is relentless in his attempts to come against it. But Jesus promised that the gates of hell would not prevail against the church (Matthew 16:18). Jesus is the Head of the church (Colossians 1:24).

Some Christians want to be free of any kind of church authority because of abuses they have seen and perhaps experienced. (If there is truly wrongdoing in a church, the Word of God gives guidelines to address and correct the problem. There may also be times when changing churches may be the best course.)

Whatever the case, every Christian is exhorted to be in a church and under apostolic authority for their welfare and the health of the church.

Today, we are blessed with many beautiful and informative documentaries on television about wildlife on the earth. Have you ever noticed what happens to gazelle or antelope when they wander away from the herd? A hungry lion or other predator may be lurking in the bush, just waiting to pounce on their next meal. The predator does not pity the young, weak, sick or the old.

Attending church regularly and staying in close relationship with other Christians is vital for our spiritual protection and development.

8 Guidelines for
A Solid Christian Church

It is essential that we fellowship in a biblically-sound church. Here are some guidelines for choosing the right church:

1. Salvation—The pastor teaches there is *only one way to be saved,* and that is by confessing and making Jesus Christ the Lord of your life (Romans 10:13).

2. The Cross—The Cross is central to our Christian walk. At the Cross, our salvation was purchased and the New Covenant was established. Are you being taught the importance of "dying to the flesh daily" and following the teachings of Jesus no matter the personal cost or sacrifice (Luke 9:23). Without the Cross, the church is dead.

3. The Blood—Some churches avoid teaching about the Blood of Jesus. Without the Blood, we have no salvation. Jesus died on the Cross and shed His precious Blood so we can have eternal life, healing and deliverance (1 Peter 1:19).

4. Repentance—The word *repent* is used in the New Testament 66 times in 60 verses. The Greek word generally means "to change one's mind." It often addresses believers who have backslidden. In Revelation 2 and 3, the churches are exhorted by Our Lord Jesus to repent or suffer the consequences. Thank God for grace, His free gift for all who trust Jesus Christ as their Lord and Savior. But God still expects us to live obedient and holy lives. It is the responsibility of church leadership to make this clear to the congregants.

5. The Word and Prayer—All Christians must study to know what the Bible says for themselves. How can we know that a minister is preaching the truth if we have not read and studied the Word of God? Each message preached by a minister must be centered on the teaching of Scripture.

Prayer is communication with the Father and greatly strengthens our Christian experience. Jesus set the example by praying continually—all night at times. Before He began His earthly ministry, Jesus spent 40 days and nights praying and fasting in the desert. Paul, the great apostle said, *"I pray without ceasing" (1 Thessalonians 5:17)*. Every church should teach and encourage the people how to study the Bible and pray strategically and effectively.

6. The Holy Spirit—The church was

born on the day of Pentecost. Fifty days after Jesus' death and ten days after His ascension into heaven, the Holy Spirit came upon the 120 disciples who were praying in the upper room. Suddenly, they were empowered to do the works of Christ like never before. The entire book of Acts is about the power of the Holy Spirit working through believers to build Jesus' church.

Some churches do not think it is necessary to preach about the power of the Holy Spirit. It has been my experience that such a church lacks the life and power of God.

7. Evangelism—The Great Commission is a command for all believers in Christ to spread the Gospel (Good News) of salvation to the world (Matthew 28:16). Every healthy church is committed to evangelism, missions and reaching out to lost and hurting souls—both in their community and all over the world.

8. Accountability—Most denominations follow an accountability structure. The church has a pastor, elders and deacons (in some churches, the titles are different but have the same significance). The office of the pastor is set forth as part of the five-fold ministry mentioned in Ephesians 4:11 and 12. The pastor and eldership is overseen by a bishop (or other designated title) as the New

Testament churches were overseen by the apostles. The church must be held to the highest possible standard of integrity, sound biblical teaching and example, morality and holy living.

Government

In 1 Timothy 2:1-3 we read, *"Therefore I exhort first of all that supplications, prayers, intercessions, and giving of thanks be made for all men, for kings and all who are in authority, that we may lead a quiet and peaceable life in all godliness and reverence."*

Many times people want to complain and criticize the government and leaders of the land. God commands us to pray for our leaders.

No one is happy when they hear a siren go off behind them, and suddenly realize they are about to get a ticket for speeding. But if a prowler is snooping around your house, there is no one you would rather see than a police officer!

God has set civil authority over us for protection and the common good. It is our duty to respect authority. If more Christians would pray, stay informed, vote and get involved in the process of government, perhaps there would be less complaints.

Citizens of nations are under their national covering no matter where they are on earth. If they are threatened, their governmental authorities will do whatever possible to protect and help them.

Even when we do not share the same beliefs as our leaders, we must respect their positions and pray for God to lead them by His Spirit in every situation.

"Honor all people, love the brotherhood. Fear God. Honor the king (1Peter 2:17).

Never Tolerate Spiritual Abuse

Unfortunately, there have been individuals who have assumed authority over people that is not scriptural. This is another reason why it is imperative to study the Word of God so that you will be able to judge. No person should ever be required to obey unjust laws or treatment which violate biblical principles, right of conscience, or Christian liberties. No person should ever be manipulated, controlled or used to advance another's desire to rule or advance themselves.

Position

Some women want to do their own thing. That is not biblical, smart or very effective. God calls us to find our place in the Body of Christ and work in cooperation with every other member. This is the only way the church can function effectively. Jesus is the Head of the church, and all of His people are part of the Body of Christ.

God has a unique position for you in his Body. Almost everyone starts in a low place, and as they prove themselves to God and leadership, they advance with more responsibility and authority. Those who seek a senior position before they are adequately prepared and seasoned by trials and experience will likely bring unnecessary pain to themselves and others. A wise woman once stated, "You must crawl before you walk!"

Christ Women, rejoice in your coverings, authorities and correct position. God is so wonderful to give us security, protection and a special place to serve.

The Foundation That Will Not Fail

The foundation of our service is our love relationship with Jesus.

Secondly, we are diligent to show ourselves approved of God, a worker who does not need to be ashamed, rightly dividing the Word of Truth. (2 Timothy 2:15).

We must become well acquainted with the full counsel of God's Holy Word.

Make the Investment

It takes 70 hours and 40 minutes to read the Bible out loud.

It takes 52 hours and 20 minutes to read the Old Testament

It takes 18 hours and 20 minutes to read the New Testament

It takes two hours and 43 minutes to read the Gospel of Luke

~11~
The Past is in the Tomb—The Future Is in Your Womb

"Do not remember the former things,
nor consider the things of old.
Behold, I will do a new thing, now it
shall spring forth; shall you not know it?
I will even make a road in the wilderness
and rivers in the desert."
~Isaiah 43:18-19~

Most women reading this book retain some painful memories from the past. Some of you have actually endured the unendurable. Others have been used, humiliated, betrayed, rejected, disappointed and cast out. No doubt, some dear sister is reading this book hoping for one last reason to live. There will also be a few—precious few—who have not experienced serious difficulties. You are secure, confident and anxious to move forward in your destiny. Whatever the case, God wants you healed, whole and assured that your life has meaning and purpose. No matter the past, He is a God who wants to give you beauty for ashes and turn every curse into a blessing.

Here is one of my favorite Scriptures that has brought me comfort and hope during the trials of life.

"Nevertheless...the Lord your God turned the curse into a blessing for you, because the Lord your God loves you" (Deuteronomy 23:5).

First of all, as a Christian, you are promised that every curse is broken off of you because of the work Christ accomplished on the Cross. The day you asked Jesus Christ to be the Lord and Savior of your life, all sins were forgiven and evil lost its power over you.

Many women—and men—do not fully know and understand the power of salvation and the liberty it brings. The past can only hurt if *you* give it the power to do so. You give it strength by thinking and talking about it. The more you refuse to forgive yourself and others, the chains around your heart tighten. They hold you captive to the past and to the enemy.

Isaiah 61:1 and Luke 4:18-19 declare that Jesus came to set the captive free. That's good news! You must be totally liberated from past baggage to move forward with faith into your victorious future. Let's address some of the chains which may be holding you back and how to break them.

1. Guilt—This is the agonizing and continual feeling of condemnation because of something you thought, said or did. You know it was wrong and despise yourself for it. It's hard to more forward because you feel unworthy. You don't love yourself and cannot fully love others. The sin you committed never leaves you and digs its claws into your soul every minute of the day.

Release—*"If we confess our sins, He is faithful and just to forgive us our sins and to cleanse us from all unrighteousness" (1 John 1:9).*

That Scripture declares—not some unrighteousness but all unrighteousness. Now that is very good news!

Right now, this very moment before you continue to the next point, stop! Sincerely and humbly go before God and ask Him to forgive every sin and failure that the Holy Spirit will bring to your remembrance. Tell Him that you repent (willfully turn from) ever committing any of those sins again. Then receive His forgiveness and cleansing. There is more good news: the Bible tells us that not only are the sins forgiven, but God casts them into a sea of forgetfulness (see Micah 7:19). Now, and in the future, do not remember or mention them anymore. If the thoughts come to your mind, immediately and deliberately refuse to meditate upon them. God has forgiven you. Forgive yourself. Take control of your mind.

I will add that if you have wronged someone, proceed to make it right if possible. If you need to apologize, ask forgiveness with a loving attitude and spirit. If the person accepts your apology, you have lost an enemy. If they do not receive your apology, you have done what you should. Leave it with God.

Return what you have stolen, restore what you have damaged if possible. Ask the Holy Spirit to give you instructions. There will be some things that have happened which cannot be revisited. If you cannot make a wrong right—or if revisiting it would make matters worse—give this to God also. Bless the people in your prayer time and move on.

2. Sexual Abuse—It never ceases to amaze me how many women have been sexually abused. I have heard so many stories of how they were violated as toddlers, children and teenagers by fathers, step-fathers, brothers, uncles and others. Women have sat before me weeping about the fear and helplessness. Many times, if they did find the courage to tell their mothers, they would either not believe them or would not address the problem. So many women have been harassed, tormented and raped—with no one to help. These women have difficulty in a marital relationship and have great struggles getting over feeling dirty, used and having no worth.

Release—*Only God can heal this festering sore, and He surely can. It was not your fault. You were a victim. The enemy of your soul will accuse you. He is a liar and the father of lies. Go to God and tell Him everything that happened and how you feel. Pour out your heart. He will not be shocked or dismayed. His great Father's love will cover and comfort you. Then fall into His everlasting arms and let Him love and heal you. Again, take control of your thoughts!*

Your body and soul were violated, but that violation can never touch who you are in Christ. You have just as much value as you did the moment the Holy Spirit gave you life in your mother's womb. You are a new creature in Christ. Old thing have passed away and all things have become new (2 Corinthians 5:17).

Jesus can truly turn your scars into stars. You are special, important and of great worth. This may be extremely difficult, but forgive the ones who hurt you and pray for God to touch their hearts and change their lives. Jesus explained that anyone can love those who love them, but it takes the grace of God to love our enemies and those who have damaged us. If someone who hurt you still tries to hurt you, it must be reported and stopped! If someone hurt you and continues to hurt others, it must be reported. Please go to your pastor to get help with this if necessary. Fully document everything that happened. Turn the tables on the devil and help others overcome the pain of their past by sharing what God has done for you.

3. Regrets—Who does not have regrets? I certainly do and they are too many to count. We all miss it and fall short. Sometimes we are downright stupid (putting it bluntly). We might have knowingly or unknowingly hurt others, missed golden opportunities or allowed ourselves to be used. The list goes on and on. It hurts to think about it. What God says to me is, "Remember Lot's wife."

In Genesis 18 and 19 we read the story of Sodom and Gomorrah's depravity. It was a city of sin and shame. There were not even ten men in the city who loved and obeyed God, so He decided to wipe it off of the face of the earth. However, there was one man of God to be found and his name was Lot, the nephew of Abraham. So the Lord, in His mercy, sent His angels to rescue Lot and his family before His fiery judgment fell. They hastily led Lot, his wife and two daughters outside of the city just in time—and they gave them this command, ***"Escape for your life! Do not look behind you...lest you be destroyed"*** *(19:17).*

Lot's wife did not obey the command and looked over her shoulder. The minute she looked back, she froze and turned to a pillar of salt. She died in her tracks.

Release*—The biblical principle is clear. When God says don't look back, don't look back. What happened cannot be erased, and there is no going back to change it. Nevertheless, you have learned from the experience and are older and wiser. Do not allow bitterness, resentment, anger and other negative emotions to grip your mind and soul. Release means letting go. Let go of the past. It's over and done with. Tomorrow is full of promise and new adventures. God gave Lot and his family new beginnings. He will give you new beginnings and opportunities also. Our obedience is all He requires.*

4. Betrayal—Betrayal hurts. It smarts.

It cuts and scars. Your trust has been violated. It can crush the soul, make you sick, and send you spiraling into depression and despair. Betrayal steals your joy, makes you angry and causes you to cry until there are no tears left. Adultery, revealing your secrets, being blatantly used for another's advantage cut to the heart. Perhaps you invested days, months and years to help someone. You loved them unconditionally, believed in them when no one else would and were there for them when no one else was—and then when life smiled upon them again, they had no more use for you.

It could be that your dad left your mother and you for another woman or venture in life. It broke your heart and left you feeling insecure, confused, unloved and unimportant. Maybe it was your mother who abandoned you for someone or something else. And then there are friends who may have stolen your ideas and claimed them for their own. Some of you have had a friend convince you to invest in a business venture and then took your money and ran.

From time to time, it happens in one form or another.

Release—*Take a deep breath. There was a prominent Christian couple. They ministered together for years and enjoyed respect and fulfillment. Multitudes* *of people were encouraged by their teachings. Then one day, the wife discovered her husband was having an affair. Disbelief! Her heart was ripped out! No, it couldn't be. But it happened.*

After her initial outburst of pain and anger, she only knew one thing to do. She ran to her Heavenly Father, the One who will "never leave you or forsake you." For her, it was the closet. She went in, fell on her knees and prayed and prayed until there were no more tears and no more prayers. She lay there. The unthinkable had befallen. She felt dead. But she would not leave the closet until she heard from God. She could choose to forgive her husband, receive godly counsel and work at rebuilding their marriage; or, she might seek vengeance by demanding a divorce and publicly humiliating her husband; or she could continue her marriage with resentment and outrage for as long as it would last. In the end, she chose the first option—forgive, get help and rebuild. Her marriage and their ministry were restored in the process of time. Yes, there were scars; but the grace, love and mercy of God prevailed.

There are times when I have been betrayed. It took me totally by surprise. It usually does. And it went deep. This is when having a strong love relationship

156

with Jesus makes all the difference. He is the Lover Who will never betray us. He will never hurt or harm us in any way. He always believes the best, keeps your confidences and loves you with a love that fills the heavens and the earth.

So, I think about His love. As long as He never fails me, I can make it. As long as I have Him, I can make it.

And then, admittedly, there have been times when I have betrayed others. Maybe I didn't mean to but it took place. Perhaps, initially, I didn't think or pray about the matter. I greatly disappointed someone who trusted me. How can I judge another? His grace is sufficient. Jesus was betrayed by His disciples and friends. Judas committed treason with a kiss, and the apostles in their unfaithfulness not only abandoned Jesus but also denied Him. Nevertheless, He freely forgave and freely loved them anyway. With God, we forgive, we heal, we even rejoice and start the next chapter of our lives.

The Baby in Your Womb

A baby starts with a seed so small it cannot be seen with the naked eye. The father's sperm penetrates the mother's microscopic egg and a miracle takes place—a new life is born. Within that tiny new person are all of the components to shape a complete man or woman. Normally, it takes about 20 years for the person to physically mature but a lifetime for all of the gifts and talents to develop—with the cooperation of the individual.

It is the same with the seeds of dreams that God places in our hearts. They start out very small, and they take time to grow and develop. At a set time, we must choose what to do with our spiritual child. We can nourish it and give it every possible advantage; or we can abort it. Abortion is not an option.

What do we mean by a "dream?" A **God dream** is a picture that He places in your mind either when you are sleeping or when you are awake. It is a vision of things He has created you to accomplish. There are also **self dreams**. Those are dreams we give ourselves of what we

158

might like to do or achieve. A self dream may or may not happen. There are no guarantees. When God gives a dream, it definitely can come to pass. If He gives you a dream, He will provide you every-thing you need to fulfill it. But thereafter you must decide if you will cooperate and pay the price for its fulfillment.

Mary Kay was born in 1915. She wit-nessed dramatic changes in the world as a result the telephone, radio, automobile, television, airplane and other wonders which were invented. She married and had three children. Disappointments came and she found herself in the position of having to raise the children alone.

In her early years, not many women ran large companies but that did not keep Mary Kay from pursuing her dream with determination, passion and hard work. In 1963, taking a huge step in faith, she invested her entire savings of $5,000 to start her own company called Mary Kay Cosmetics.

A deeply religious woman, she lived by the Golden Rule, *"Do unto others as you have them do unto you."* She combined this rule with her priorities: "God first, family second and career third. As she trusted God and sought to live by His Word, He blessed her beyond her biggest dreams. Before her passing in 2001, her company enjoyed sales of over $3 billion dollars annually with some 3,500 employees and over one million independent beauty consultants. She believed in rewarding hard work and along with many other gifts awarded over 80,000 pink Cadillacs and other cars to her top achievers. One of her chief executives who had become a millionaire said, "She helped me to believe that I could be anything in the world that I could ever believe of becoming."

The story has been told that when television's "60 Minutes" Morley Safer interviewed Mary Kay Ash, he asked her if she was using God. She answered, "I sincerely hope not. I hope instead that God is using me."

"Shall I bring to the time of birth, and not cause delivery?" (Isaiah 66:9).

What dream has God placed in your heart? Don't let it die. Think and pray about it. Explore the possibilities. Take a step in faith.

Your dream is waiting to come true!

~12~
How to Plant and Grow Your Ministry

"Love God and Love People"
~River City Love Squad, Louisville, KY~

5 Ways to Plant Your Ministry

1. What is in your hand?—Moses had been on the "backside of the desert" for 40 years—banished from Egypt—after murdering an Egyptian who was persecuting an Israelite. He had most likely given up any dreams of great accomplishments in his life. However, when he least expected it, God Almighty appeared to him in a burning bush and commanded Moses to go back to Egypt and set the Israelites free. Moses was astounded and doubted his ability to do so. He questioned God:

"O my Lord, I am not eloquent, neither before nor since. You have spoken to Your

servant; but I am slow of speech and slow of tongue.' So the Lord said to him, 'Who has made man's mouth? Or who makes the mute, the deaf, the seeing, or the blind? Have not I, the Lord? Now therefore, go, and I will be with your mouth and teach you what you shall say'" (Exodus 4:10-12).

God told Moses what he needed to hear. If I AM THAT I AM gives you divine instructions, do not argue with Him or offer excuses. God asked Moses what he held in his hand. Moses answered, *"A rod," (v. 2).* God proceeded to turn the rod into a serpent which greatly frightened Moses and he ran from it. Then God commanded Moses to pick up the serpent by the tail. Moses obediently grabbed the tail of the snake, and lo—it turned back into a rod. From then on, Moses kept his rod with him, and God used it to demonstrate many mighty miracles.

What is in *your* hand? Do you want to teach and preach? What opening is available to you now? If no one is inviting you to speak, then speak where you can: a Bible study in your home, teaching children's church or even on a street corner. Be faithful in little, and God will increase your opportunities as you prove yourself trustworthy.

Do you want to open a home for abused women and help them get a new start in life? You may have to begin by assisting someone else even in the most menial manner. You will learn many valuable lessons—and one of the most important lessons is that God's servants must be humble, teachable and obedient. Whatever you can do, do it with all of your heart. God will advance you in due season.

Perhaps, you have been called to be a minister through your vocation: a physician, grocery store clerk, attorney, banker, computer technician, graphic designer or a salesperson. Ministry is every- where; and representatives of Christ are needed everywhere.

Some mistakenly think they can only be a minister if ordained and working on a church staff. The truth is, all Christians are called to be ministers. So, look at where you are and evaluate how you can use your current situation to show others the love and salvation of Jesus.

2. Continually pray and seek direction—Without Him, you can do nothing. And nothing is more important than your time with the Lord. Meet with Him each day for a time of prayer and Bible study. He will empower you and give you instructions.

Jesus was and is the Son of God, and He gave prayer first priority in His life.

He often rose up early in the morning while it was yet night and went out to a secluded place and communed with the Father. Before important decisions were made, such as selecting His 12 disciples, He spent the entire night in prayer. Jesus drew His strength from the Father and set an example for His followers.

3. Be willing to take one step at a time—A baby doesn't begin walking the day he or she is born. Learning to walk is a process. Babies must grow up. At approximately eight months of age, the baby will venture out by crawling—at first very slowly, gaining momentum and strength. A few months later, the big day arrives. While mom and dad coax and encourage, the baby takes his or her first steps in faith confident that loving hands are within reach.

It's the same way in the ministry. We do not jump from "start" to "finish" in one day. It's a process. Be patient. There will be many tests and trials of your faith. You will be proven in the fire of the Holy Spirit. It's not because God is a hard Father. He does not want you to get into a situation that you are unprepared to handle.

4. Seek guidance from your pastor and mentor—A good place to start any kind of ministry is right in your home church.

You will be a blessing and be blessed in return. Your pastor will be an invaluable aid to you. Prior to discussing your calling with him, get your thoughts together. Condense—on one sheet of paper—your calling (the dream God has given you), experience, mission and vision statements. Print out a neat copy for your meeting with him. At that time, you will share your heart and ask for his direction. Be prepared to tell him how your ministry will be a blessing to the church. If he offers you counsel that might not be exactly what you are hoping for, be willing to follow his advice. He may even ask you to wait for awhile until you have more training and experience. You may have to make some adjustments. There is also the possibility that your pastor will ask his associate or another minister in the church to talk with you first. Whatever the case, show your appreciation and follow their advice with a respectful and good attitude. God will bless you for honoring and appreciating church leadership.

5. Network with others who are successful—There is an old saying that "birds of a feather flock together." You cannot sit at home and wait for the phone to ring or a message from cyberspace. Hear me well. You will sit and wait forever. You must become proactive and make it a top priority to spend as much time as possible with other ministers and Christian women. Seek out those who share the same burden. Walk along with them, watch, learn and help them. You will gain wisdom and insight. You will learn the slow and good way instead of the fast and painful way. As an added blessing—as mentioned in other sections of this book—the anointing of the Holy Spirit upon them will begin to come upon you.

All successful Christians are connected with many other people who share the same vision and goals. If you are shy, you will have to get over it to move forward with God's call on your life. Shyness is not humility. Shyness is nothing but fear of failure or what other people think. Or, it could be due to your never having been around many people. Possibly, you are insecure because of past disappointments or improper nurturing from your parents or others in authority. You can and must overcome timidity and shyness to be effective in reaching out to others with the love of God. He will help you overcome fear and move forward in faith as you trust in Him.

I speak from experience having been extremely shy as a new Christian.

After months of staying in the shadows, the Lord spoke to my heart and said, "If you love me, you will do this." So, I had to move forward in faith. It was excruciating at times, but God never let me down. If God speaks, you must obey at all cost. The Scripture that set me free is: *"For God has not given us a spirit of fear, but of power and of love and of a sound mind" (2 Timothy 1:7).*

5 Ways to Grow Your Ministry

1. Plant a seed—Planting a seed refers to many areas of life which includes giving. The Bible repeatedly teaches to plant seeds in order to grow, mature and harvest. If we give love, we will receive love; if we are friendly, we will have friends.

Whatever service you are called to by the Lord, pray about what kind of a seed you can plant for an increase. It could be helping another person who is serving in the same kind of outreach. The help may be physical or financial. The heart of the Gospel is giving. God planted His Son, Jesus Christ, on the earth for the salvation of a multitude of sinners, *"For*

God so loved the world, that He gave His only begotten Son, that whoever believes in Him should not perish but have everlasting life" (John 3:16).

2. Do everything "as unto the Lord"— Why do you want to serve the Lord? Is it for Him and Him alone? When you start serving God, there will be many times when no one will know but Him. Will that matter to you? There will be times when you will not be thanked or appreciated for what you do. You might not be paid. It may be that others who labor less than you receive greater recognition. If you are on a staff, they may receive greater compensation. The enemy might whisper in your ear, "it's not fair!" Resentment and anger will try to take root in your heart. Here is the secret to peace:

"And whatever you do, do it heartily, as to the Lord and not to men, knowing that from the Lord you will receive the reward of the inheritance; for you serve the Lord Christ" (Colossians 3:23-24).

God sees it all and He is your Source. He will reward you at the right time. And those who knowingly take advantage of you will give an account for their actions. If they cheat you, they will reap what they have sown. Therefore, I repeat—is it for Him and Him alone? Constantly check your motives.

Whatever you do, whether it is cleaning the sanctuary, feeding the homeless and needy, visiting the jail or nursing home or hospital, do your very best for the Lord. Serve them as you would serve Christ and He will bless you.

There may be times when you should address unfair situations; but make sure that you do so after prayer and with the right spirit.

3. Delegate—It is difficult to grow without help. It was never God's intention for us to do the work of the Kingdom by ourselves. When Moses led the children of Israel through the desert, he was overwhelmed with judging the people from morning until night. Finally, his father-in-law, Jethro, gave him valuable advice. He told Moses to appoint worthy leaders of ten, fifty, one-hundred and one-thousand to judge the people, and they were to bring only the difficult matters to Moses. Moses gratefully followed his father-in-law's advice and his burden was not only lessened but the people received help more readily (Exodus 18). Include others in your ministry as much as possible.

4. Be diligent and persistent—Do what others will not. Solomon, the wisest man who ever lived (other than Christ) said it well: *"The soul of a lazy man desires, and has nothing; but the soul of the diligent shall be made rich" (Proverbs 13:4).*

There is another word for lazy people and that is what my husband calls "slackers." Slackers often talk boastfully but they do not produce much. They love to take credit for what other people do—and try to get others to carry their weight as much as possible. If nothing gets them out of an assignment that calls for too much effort, they will begin to criticize leadership and complain behind their backs. Here is what I have observed. The slacker eventually is found out and loses an opportunity to glorify God in his or her work.

What is diligence? It is putting your mind to an assignment and doing everything possible to complete it with excellence. It may mean getting up early, working late and giving up some pleasure in your spare time. A diligent person is dependable and efficient and will not only receive favor from the Lord but favor from their fellow laborers and leadership. They will advance, because they are needed and appreciated. A sold-out Christ Woman never gives up. If she doesn't succeed the first time, she tries again...and again...and again. *"I press toward the goal for the prize of the*

upward call of God in Christ Jesus"
(Philippians 3:14).

5. Stay in your fast lane—These five words are some of the best advice I ever received. They were spoken to me by an elder in my church, R. W. Fawbush. There may be many things that you can do pretty well and some things in which you excel. But what can you do better than anybody else? Have you heard the old saying, "A jack of all trades and a master of none?"

Another good piece of advice I received as a young minister was from the wife of my first pastor, Fern Rodgers, "Never try to be someone else. Just be yourself the best you can be." Dear heart, if you love to counsel, don't try to be a jail minister. If you are a gifted teacher, don't attempt to preach like an evangelist every time you have an opportunity. Leaders don't usually make the best administrators; and administrators often wonder why no one is following them. **Do not judge yourself by another's accomplishments; and do not judge others by your accomplishments**.

My husband is a lay minister but he is also a builder. If I tried to construct a house I would be a total failure. However, I can cook a pot of chicken and dumplings that my husband could never begin to cook himself.

Be assured, there are numerous situations wherein you are specially equipped to fulfill God's purposes. God will assist you to carry out His plan. God expects His people to pitch in and work together. Use wisdom. Do what needs to be done with a good team spirit and attitude. However, when possible **"stay in your fast lane."**

Watch Out for the Green-Eyed Monster

"O, beware, my lord of jealousy!" Shakespeare wrote, for *"it is the green-eyed monster which doth mock the meat it feeds on."*

If you ever feel envy or resentment stirring in your heart because another woman or minister gets more attention and appreciation than you, nip it in the bud! That's what started the process of satan getting kicked out of heaven! Rejoice when someone else is being used by God.

I have observed ministers who have tried to keep others from opportunities because they did not want to be up-staged or replaced. This is devilish, and the result may be that the person who holds back another may lose what they have. Seek the low place and never exalt yourself.

"Humble yourselves [feeling very insignificant] in the presence of the Lord, and He will exalt you [He will lift you up and make your lives significant]" (James 4:10 AMP).

There may come a day when you will recognize that others are jealous of the way God uses you. When you become aware of this, begin praying for the person with the problem. When God gives you a special anointing, you can probably expect some jealousy. Do not take their attitude and comments personally.

Guard Your Motives

I have observed ministers who appeared to have one thing on their agenda: Me, Me, Me and more Me. They continually draw attention to themselves and constantly rehearse all of their ministry opportunities and accomplishments to anyone who will listen. A mature Christian desires all attention to be on Christ and will brag on Him and not themselves.

If we are seeking to build our own kingdom, get rich through the ministry, gain attention and power, it's time to repent and ask God for forgiveness. Our only motive should be to glorify the Lord Jesus Christ and do His works.

In Genesis 11 we read how all of the earth was still one language, and the people came together to build the first great city in the land of Shinar. And they said, *"Come let us build ourselves a city, and a tower, whose top is in the heavens; **let us make a name for ourselves...***" (v. 4). The outcome of their prideful venture was the destruction of the Tower of Babel and the people's language was confused. They were dispersed across the earth.

John the Baptist spoke with revelation and wisdom: ***"He must increase and I must decrease"*** (John 3:30).

The Sounding Brass and The Tinkling Cymbal

There is something I have witnessed often that I know deeply grieves the heart of God. It is when the sisters become divided and hold resentment and unforgiveness due to offence or other difficulties. Since it takes the entire Body of Christ laboring together to be effective, separations bring weakness, a negative witness to the world and delight to the enemy of our souls.

Families will always have issues from time to time. There will be misunderstandings, pressures and sometimes arguments. Parents and siblings may grow angry toward one another. But true love conquers all. The family that is committed to one another will face every challenge with God's help and work out the problems. Families are bound together forever by their blood. It is the same with God's family. There can be strife and contentions at times. But that does not mean the end of the family. God's family is bound together by the Blood of Jesus Christ. When God puts people together, it is for an eternity.

Paul heard about the division between two women in the Philippian church and addressed it in his letter:

"I implore Euodia and I implore Syntyche to be of the same mind in the Lord. And I urge you also, true companion, help these women who labored with me in the gospel...with the rest of my fellow workers, whose names are in the Book of Life. Rejoice in the Lord always. Again I will say rejoice! Let your gentleness be known to all men. The Lord is at

hand" (4:1-5).

We have to be on guard regarding the wiles of the devil, stay "prayed up" and watchful regarding the little foxes that would come in to destroy God's vine.

Dear sisters, if another sister in the Lord Jesus vexes you in any way, God's Word clearly commands you to love her and pray for her anyway. If there is an area that causes you frustration, anger, resentment or even jealousy, you must address it if you want to keep the anointing of the Holy Spirit and please the Lord.

Carnal Christians may vent hurt feelings by talking to other people at great length about perceived wrongs. They may avoid or even ignore the woman who has offended them. I have seen women hold up their noses, throw their heads back and march away from a chance to grow in the love and grace of God. Mature and selfless Christians go to the Father and pour their hearts out to Him to get victory over the situation. Here is what we should do when facing such contention.

First, do not allow yourself to criticize or discredit the woman. Stay quiet until you are under control. Pray earnestly and fervently for the sister until you have peace. Then, if at all possible, arrange a meeting with her. Get together in love and pray with one another before addressing the problem. You might say, "We are both women of God and love Jesus. We are both trying to serve Him with all of our hearts. The enemy would like to win in this situation. But we will not let that happen. We can work this out with the Father's help."

Then proceed by *gently* taking turns to say what is bothering you—frankly and truthfully. Do not accuse, offer excuses, blame someone else or sidetrack the issue. Listen to your sister, put yourself in her shoes. Try to understand. Ask one another for forgiveness. Pray for one another. Hug each other and defeat the devil!

"If [I can] speak in the tongues of men, and [even] of angels, but have not love (that reasoning, intentional, spiritual devotion such as is inspired by God's love for and in us), I am only a noisy gong or a clanging cymbal...Love endures long and is patient and kind; love never is envious nor boils over with jealousy, is not boastful or vainglorious, does not display itself haughtily. It is not conceited (arrogant and inflated with pride); it is not rude (unmannerly) and does not act unbecomingly...Love never fails..." (1 Corinthians 13:1-8 AMP).

Plant your ministry in the soil of love and it will prosper forever.

~13~
Beautiful Bride
Of Christ

*"Some glad day, all watching past, You
will come for me at last..."*
~Unknown~

*"Let us be glad and rejoice and give Him
glory, for the marriage of the Lamb has
come, and His wife has made herself
ready. And to her it was granted to be
arrayed in fine linen, clean and bright, for
the fine linen is the righteous acts of the
saints. Then he said to me, 'Write:
blessed are those who are called to the
marriage supper of the Lamb'" (Revelation
19:7-10).*

The dream of being a bride someday
thrills the heart of almost every little girl.
From the time she is a guest at her first
wedding, she begins to imagine what her
wedding will be like someday. She envisions wearing the most beautiful white
dress of all time. An exquisite veil will
flow from the crown of her head, past her
shoulders and down her back. Leaning

on the strong arm of her beaming and stately father, she will walk slowly up the aisle toward her knight in shining white armor. All of the guests will be filled with admiration.

When her gallant groom sees her gracefully walking toward him at last, his eyes will shine with happiness. She will gaze back at him through misty eyes full of love, devotion and anticipation of a happy life with the man of her dreams.

Marriage is holy in the eyes of God. It is so sacred that it represents the soon-coming marriage of Jesus Christ to His Bride—the redeemed, saved, born-again saints who have entrusted their lives to Him forever.

Christians are so in love with Jesus that they can barely wait for the Marriage Supper of the Lamb. Just as an earthly bride longs for her wedding day, the Bride of Christ aches to be joined with her holy Husband.

"As the deer pants for the water brooks, so pants my soul for You, O God. My soul thirsts for God, for the living God..." (Psalm 42:11-2a).

Scripture tells us that this celestial celebration will occur at the end of the seven years of Tribulation, right before Jesus Christ returns to earth with His bride to establish His kingdom on the earth. When everyone has been saved who will be saved, when the last martyr has laid down his or her life for the Gospel, when God's judgment is just about complete, the Bride of Christ will gather for the greatest feast of all time! Jesus told His disciples at the Last Supper:

"But I say to you, I will not drink of this fruit of the vine from now on until that day which I drink it new with you in My Father's Kingdom" (Matthew 26:29).

Concerning the last days and what will happen in the final seven years, before Jesus returns to earth with His bride, different scholars have contrasting understandings of prophetic Scriptures. A considerable number of eschatology (study of end-time prophecy) students believe that the Rapture of the church will occur at least seven years before the Second Coming of Jesus Christ. This is the author's view. But if other Christians hold different interpretations, let us not be divided. What is important is that we all look forward to being joined with Christ at the end of our lives and always are prepared to meet Him.

(Note: For those who have not studied

Jesus Christ calls His bride up into the air to meet Him before God's great wrath is poured out on rebellious mankind. See 1 Corinthians 15:51-52; 1 Thessalonians 4:13-18).

The Second Coming is at the end of God's judgment, when Jesus comes back to earth with His bride and the holy angels to defeat the antichrist, false prophet and his armies at the Battle of Armageddon (Revelation 19). At the conclusion of this battle, the antichrist, the false prophet and all of those who took the mark of the beast, 666, will be cast into the Lake of Fire forever and ever. Satan will be locked in the bottomless pit for 1,000 years until his time of reckoning comes. The Bride of Christ will settle in Jerusalem with her Bridegroom Jesus Christ. The saints will rebuild the beautiful City of Zion, and they will rule and reign with Him for all of eternity! (See author's book, REVELATION for more teaching on end times.)

The following is an explanation of the ancient Jewish wedding and how it modeled the betrothal and marriage of Jesus Christ and His bride. As you read this Jewish history, you will understand another reason why a great multitude of believers expect the Rapture to occur at any time—and at least seven years before the Second Coming.

The Betrothal

In ancient Jewish times, either a young may or his parents decided upon a young woman who would make a good wife. The prospective bridegroom would build his courage and visit the home of the young woman and express his desire to her parents. If her parents agreed that he would be a suitable husband for their daughter, they would negotiate the price (mohair) of the bride. If the bridegroom was able to pay the price, the contract was made. To seal their contract, the bride and groom drank together from a cup of wine. From that moment on the couple were regarded as husband and wife, but there would be a time of preparation before they could come together as husband and wife and consummate the marriage.

Jesus Christ paid for His bride at Calvary. The cup of wine shared by the betrothed couple symbolized the future Blood Jesus would shed on the Cross to save man from their sins. He paid the greatest price of all time for His beloved. "*...To Him who loved us and washed us* *from our sins in His own blood..." (Revelation 1:5b).*

The Preparation

After the sealing of the marriage covenant, the bridegroom returned to his father's house to prepare a place for his bride. As he worked on their future home, his bride took time to prepare a trousseau for the wedding. This is a type and picture of the way Jesus has carefully been preparing a special dwelling place for His bride. At the same time, His bride prepares herself to meet her Groom face to face with much anticipation.

"...In My Father's house are many mansions (dwelling places); if it were not so, I would have told you. If I go to prepare a place for you. I will come again and receive you to Myself; that where I am, there you may be also" (John 14:1-3 Explanation in parenthesis by author).

The Watching

According to tradition, the bridegroom would come back for his bride in the middle of the night—after their new home was ready. The best man and other male escorts would excitedly accompany him to claim his bride. The bride had been preparing herself and knew he would come for her—but the exact night was kept secret. She had to be ready at all times so she would not be caught unprepared and miss his coming.

As the bridegroom and his friends approached her home, the young men would shout and sound a shofar (a ram's horn). The bride and her attendants would hasten to get dressed and run out to meet the bridegroom. In Matthew 25, Jesus warned His followers to be ready for His sudden coming for them:

"The kingdom of heaven shall be likened to ten virgins who took their lamps and went out to meet the bridegroom. Now five of them were wise; and five were foolish. Those who were foolish took their lamps and took no oil with them, but the wise took oil in their vessels with their lamps. But while the bridegroom was delayed, they all slumbered and slept. And at midnight a cry was heard: 'Behold the bridegroom is coming; go out to meet him!' Then all those virgins arose and trimmed their lamps. And the foolish said to the wise, 'Give us some of your oil for our lamps are going out.' But the wise

answered, saying, 'No, lest there should not be enough for us and you; but go rather to those who sell, and buy for yourselves.' An while they went to buy, the bridegroom came, and those who were ready went in with him to the wedding; and the door was shut. Afterward the other virgins came also, saying, Lord, Lord, open to us!' But he answered and said, 'Assuredly, I say to you, I do not know you.'"

All of the virgins represent the Bride of Christ. The oil is a type of the Holy Spirit. Some of the virgins were not diligent to keep themselves ready for their Lord and missed the wedding. Those who kept themselves ready and their lamps full of oil were prepared to go when the shout was sounded.

In 1 Thessalonians 4:16-17, we read these joyful words, "For the Lord Himself will descend from heaven with a shout, with the voice of an archangel, and with the trumpet of God. And the dead in Christ will rise first. Then we who are alive and remain shall be caught up together with them in the clouds to meet the Lord in the air. And thus we shall always be with the Lord."

Dear ones, don't ever look back at the world from whence you have been delivered. Don't ever compromise your faith a chance on not having your lamp full of oil when the Bridegroom calls for His bride!

"Watch, therefore, and pray always that you may be counted worthy to escape all these things that come to pass, and to stand before the Son of Man" (Luke 21:36).

The Bridal Chamber

When the bridal party arrived at the home of the groom's father (where he had prepared a place for his bride), they found guests anxiously awaiting and ready to celebrate. The happy couple was joyously escorted to their huppah (the bridal chamber). While they consummated their marriage in privacy, the wedding party waited for the groom to make the announcement that their union was complete.

After hearing the good news, the wedding party continued to feast for seven days while the newlyweds stayed in the huppah behind a closed door. When the seven days were complete, the happy groom brought his bride out for everyone to see.

It is quite possible that the seven days of the huppah represent the seven years of God's judgment upon the earth commonly called the Tribulation. The bride was kept out of view until the set time. The Word of God clearly states that He has not appointed His children to the wrath of His judgment.

"For God did not appoint us to wrath, but to obtain salvation through our Lord Jesus Christ, who died for us, that whether we wake or sleep, we should live together with Him" (1 Thessalonians 5:9).

Also, it is interesting to note that the seven years of Tribulation are detailed between Chapters 6 and 19 in the book of Revelation, and the church (bride) is not mentioned one time during the judgments of that time period.

Thank God for His bridal chamber, located in heaven. What a day that will be when our union with Jesus Christ will be made complete.

The Celebration

The bride and groom and all of the wedding party celebrated during the seven days of huppah. But that was only the beginning of the newlyweds life together. After the guests left, their marriage began. Everyday they learned more about each other and shared more intimacy. The groom proudly presented her with a new home which he prepared with his own hands. She presented her trousseau which included lovely clothing along with the items they needed to make their house a home. Previously they had been two individuals; now they were one in the sight of God.

"I held him and would not let him go" (Song of Solomon 3:4a).

Christ Woman, perhaps you have been disappointed many times during your lifetime. It is possible that you have endured pain and rejection that only God can heal. In the days of your journey on this earth, you have experienced rain and sunshine, defeat and victory, rejection and acceptance. Some dreams came true and others did not.

Praise God, the day is coming—the glorious, triumphant and long-awaited day is coming—when you will see Him face to face. He will heal every wound and erase the painful memories. You will experience love as you have never known it before. You will take residence in the beautiful place He has prepared for you alone.

Your heart will rejoice and be satisfied

in His love forever!

"Eye has not seen, nor ear heard, nor has it entered into the heart of man the things which God has prepared for those who love Him" (1 Corinthians 2:9).

"And behold, I am coming quickly, and My reward is with Me, to give to everyone according to his work. I am the Alpha and the Omega, the Beginning and the End, the First and the Last...And the Spirit and the bride say, 'Come!' And let him who hears say, 'Come!' And let him who thirsts come..." (Revelation 22:13 -17).

> Some glad day, all watching past,
> You will come for me at last;
> Then I'll see you, hear your voice,
> Be with you, with you rejoice;
> How the sweet hope
> thrills me through,
> Sets me wearying for you.
>
> ~Unknown~

We Would See Jesus

Oh, to see that precious face!
To feel His wonderful, secure embrace!
What joy! Knowing I am in Heaven at last!
The Valley of Woe is past, is past.

Oh glory! Kneeling at His feet!
Covering them with kisses warm and sweet.
Tears flow over the age old scars
That bled profusely on wooden bars.

For me! For me! Years ago.
For all mankind, the love He showed.
The bravery, gentleness, truth and Blood
Made white as snow our brotherhood.

Dear Jesus, Sweet Jesus, My Savior all,
How my heart races at your every call!
The nearness of you, to have it, I must!
My heart is in your Hands...
I trust! I trust!

Rapture

Oh Jesus, if only You would come tonight
And, rescue us out of our worldly plight.
Let the trumpet sound and the angels shout.
May dead bodies from the grave come out!

Oh, what a glorious time it will be
When finally King Jesus we will see.
His face will be radiant, glowing like the sun.
Beams of light shining forth from the Holy
One.
"Come quickly Lord Jesus!"

~14~
Born Again for Greatness and Multiplication

"O to be saved from myself, dear Lord,
O to be lost in Thee,
O that it might be no more I,
But Christ, that lives in me."
~Ada A. F. Whiddington~

This book is written for the woman who has met Jesus Christ at some time in her life and trusted Him as Lord and Savior. Maybe it was during a children's Sunday school class. Or it could have been on her mother or father's knee. Perhaps she didn't meet Him until later in life when she cried out for help in a moment of desperation. Whatever the case, when she came face to face with the Savior and she fell into His outstretched arms whispering, "Yes, I am yours forever"—at that moment, she became a Christ Woman.

However, there may be a dear one reading this book who has only heard about Jesus but has never come to know Him personally. There is a possibility that you have never heard the way to be born again. After reading this book, the Holy Spirit is stirring your heart, and you know that you do not want to live one more day of your life without Jesus at your side. As you read the following Scriptures and instructions, open up your heart to receive Jesus today. You will never regret it!

HOW TO BE BORN AGAIN

"Most assuredly I say to you, unless one is born again, he cannot see the King-dom of God" (John 3:3).

We Are _Not_ Born Again By:

- Church membership
- Parent or spouse's relationship with God
- Water baptism (without salvation)
- Good works or "being good"
- Any other name other than Christ's

We Are Born Again By:

- **Grace**—It is the free gift of God. *"For by grace you have been saved through faith; and that not of yourselves; it is the gift of God and not of works, lest anyone should boast"* *(Ephesians 2:8-9).*
- **Jesus' Blood**—He took your place and my place on the Cross *"...you were not redeemed with corruptible things like silver or gold...but with the precious Blood of Christ..."* *(1 Peter 1:19).*
- **Confessing Jesus Christ as Lord**—With your mouth. *"For with the heart, one believeth unto righteousness, but with the mouth, confession is made unto salvation"* *(Romans 1:10).*

Prayer of Salvation

Father, I need you and I want your Son, Jesus Christ, to be my Lord and Savior. I believe that Jesus died on the Cross to pay the price for my sins and that He rose from the grave in triumph on the third day.

I have sinned many times in my life

and fallen short. Please forgive me of all sin and wrong doing and wash me clean with the Blood of Jesus.

Dear Jesus, I open the door of my heart to you now. I accept your invitation with great humility and thanksgiving. Come into my heart and be my Lord and Savior forever. I give you the throne of my heart with all of my soul and all of my mind and all of my being. Help me to live for you the rest of my life. In Jesus' Name I pray. Amen.

_____   _____
Your Name   Date

The Next Steps

- Find a Bible-believing church and become a member. Attend on a regular basis.
- Pray and read the Bible every day.
- Tell others what Christ has done for you.
- Make friends with strong Christians who can encourage you in the Lord.
- Turn from anyone or anything that would draw you away from the Lord.

"I, even I, am He who blots out your transgressions for My own sake; and I will not remember your sins" (Isaiah 43:25).

Multiplication

Once a person is born again by the Spirit of God, they have the power to reproduce spiritually. The book of Acts is all about people being saved, filled with the Holy Spirit and going out to share the good news of salvation with every one possible.

On the day of Pentecost, 120 disciples were in the upper room praying. They were heartbroken Jesus was no longer with them. Nevertheless, He had promised He would send His Holy Spirit to empower them to do greater works than He had done (John 14:12). They patiently waited, and He did not disappoint His disciples.

"When the Day of Pentecost had fully come, they were all with one accord in one place. And suddenly, there came a sound from heaven, as of a rushing mighty wind, and it filled the whole house where they were sitting. Then there appeared to them divided tongues of fire, And one sat upon each of them. And they were all

were all filled with the Holy Spirit and be-gan to speak with other tongues, as the Spirit gave them utterance" (Acts 2:1-4).

Immediately, the disciples were baptized in the Holy Spirit and began praising and worshipping God. It was 9:00 in the morning and the windows were open. Thousands of worshippers—many from other countries—were in Jerusalem for the feast and crowded the streets below. They heard the disciples praying in their own language and were amazed. The crowd gathered below the windows and accused the disciples of being drunk. Peter, who had been so afraid that he denied Christ three times just 50 days before, boldly presented himself to the assembly and preached Jesus Christ with the power of God. They grew silent and listened to every word. He told them, *"For these are not drunk as you supposed, since it is only the third hour of the day..." (Acts 2:15).*

At the conclusion of Peter's message, 3,000 souls were born into the Kingdom of God (2:41). From that point on, the church grew rapidly. All of the disciples went forth and spread the Gospel with signs and wonders following.

The book of Acts did not end 2,000 years ago, it is still going on today. God's people are continually being filled with the Holy Spirit and preaching the Good News that Jesus saves, delivers and heals.

Christ Woman, there are hundreds, thousands and millions of souls waiting to hear the Gospel. If you do not "go and tell" what Jesus has done for you, many will be doomed to hell.

Don't say you can't. Yes, you can! Witnessing isn't pressuring others to accept Christ. It is telling others what Christ has done for you. Ministering is all about total surrender, total servitude and total unconditional love.

Mary was just a "regular" Jewish maiden with no special credentials. But one day an angel appeared to her with a divine assignment. It seemed incredible. It was impossible in the natural. She humbly responded: *"Behold the maid-servant of the Lord! Let it be to me according to your word" (Luke 1:38).*

The rest is history. What are you waiting for?

"WHATEVER HE SAYS TO YOU DO IT!" (John 2:5)

About the Author

Joe and Diana Scheich

Diana surrendered her heart to Jesus Christ in December 1970. She and her husband, Joe, have served the Lord together since their marriage in 1972. In 2002, they founded Go Tell Ministries, Inc., a non-profit, 501(c)(3) corporation, for the purpose of spreading the Gospel around the world through missions, shortwave, printed material, their website and every means possible.

Diana feels a sense of responsibility to share her years of experience with less-experienced women who have answered God's call to reach out of themselves to others with the love of Christ.

Diana and Joe have three children, two daughters-in-law, one son-in-law and five grandchildren who are the loves of their lives.

To God be the glory,
great things He has done.
So loved He the world
that He gave us His Son,
Who yielded His life an
atonement for sin,
and opened the life gate
that all may go in.
~Fanny Crosby~

Other Books by Diana

RAPTURE
JESUS IS COMING
HEAVEN OR HELL
40 DAYS OF PRAYER & FASTING
HOLY FIRE
THE FEAR & THE GLORY OF GOD
REVELATION

To order more books:

Web: www.gotellministries.org
Email: gotellministries@twc.com

Resources

DAUGHTERS OF THE CHURCH
Ruth A. Tucker and Walter Liefeld

EXCELLENCE IN MINISTRY
Rob Thompson

FASCINATING WOMANHOOD
Helen Andelin

HOW TO BE LIKE WOMEN
OF EXCELLENCE
Pat and Ruth Williams

THE TOP 100 WOMEN OF
THE CHRISTIAN FAITH
Jewell Johnson

WHAT QUEEN ESTHER KNEW
Connie Glaser and Barbara Smalley

A DIARY OF SIGNS AND WONDERS
Maria Woodworth-Etter

YOU WILL NEVER BE THE SAME
Basilea Schlink

CURE OF ALL ILLS
Mary Stewart, Ph.D.

ENCYCLOPEDIA OF 7700
ILLUSTRATIONS
Paul Lee Tan

JEALOUSY
R. T. Kendall

SECRETS TO SPIRITUAL POWER
Watchman Nee

STREAMS IN THE DESERT—1
Mrs. Charles E. Cowman

A CHANCE TO DIE
The Life and Legacy of Amy Carmichael
Elizabeth Elliot

Endorsements

The enemy has stolen long enough from women who have a calling to the ministry. The time is now for answers, and this extraordinary book written by Diana Scheich will help untold women take leaps forward in achieving their destiny.

I have been close to Diana and her husband, Joe, for years and have seen firsthand how God has used her to see lives changed. As a woman in ministry, she knows the challenges, the tears, and the joys women face in their callings. I watched her operate in excellence as my Associate Pastor for many years. She met each day of ministry with excitement and zeal to help me, the staff and the church.

While women are more active in the ministry today than ever before, they still face opposition and challenges that men in their same roles do not face. As a Senior Pastor, I have always attempted to encourage women to answer the calling God has placed on their lives.

You are important to the Kingdom, and your gift will make room for you. You can be an exceptional wife, mother and minister. Don't ever give up on your dream.

As you read these inspired words, you will be encouraged as never before. Your greatest days are not behind you, but you are about to step through the door that will lead you to your destiny. Psalm 102:13 says, *"...For the time to favor her, yes, the set time has come."* This is your hour, your season, your set time for all God has planned for you! You will never be the same!

Steve Turpin, Sr. Pastor
Trinity World Outreach Center
Louisville, Kentucky

CHRIST WOMAN is a clear clarion call to ladies who have a deep desire to become the women God designed them to be. Words of renewal, redemption and revelation flow from Diana Scheich as she shares a storehouse of knowledge acquired from 40 years of ministry to women. Experience and revelation are a dynamite duo. Be blessed as you read. I highly recommend CHRIST WOMAN.

Pastor Greg Carter
Grace Tabernacle Assembly of God
Elizabeth, Indiana

As a pioneer for women in ministry, Diana Scheich has paved the way for women to fulfill their ministry calling. Her passion for the Word of God, along with the spirit of excellence, has sent her around the world with the Gospel of Jesus Christ. Through abundant revelation and years of experience, she knows the peaks and valleys of minis-try—especially for women. Diana shares wisdom, knowledge and truth in this book. It is a must have manual for every woman in ministry.."

Rev. Stephanie Lawson
Founder of Bridge Ministries and EWIM
(Exceptional Women in Ministry)
Louisville, Kentucky

Melissa and I have known Sister Diana Scheich over 26 years, and I will tell you that she is one of the greatest woman of God that we know! Her heart burns for lost souls and for people to draw closer to Jesus Christ in these last days! I know that her new book, CHRIST WOMAN, will set all the ladies on fire to do Kingdom work! This book is a must read!

Pastors Mike and Melissa Miller
Family Day Ministries
Louisville, Kentucky